THE
GROWING
LEADER:
healthy essentials
for children's ministry

Flagship church resources

from Group Publishing

Innovations From Leading Churches

Flagship Church Resources are your shortcut to innovative and effective leadership ideas. You'll find ideas for every area of church leadership, including pastoral ministry, adult ministry, youth ministry, and children's ministry.

Flagship Church Resources are created by the leaders of thriving, dynamic, and trend-setting churches around the country. These nationally recognized teaching churches host regional leadership conferences and are respected by other pastors and church leaders because their approaches to ministry are so effective. These flagship church resources reveal the proven ideas, programs, and principles that these churches have put into practice.

Flagship Church Resources currently available:

- *60 Simple Secrets Every Pastor Should Know*
- *The Perfectly Imperfect Church: Redefining the "Ideal Church"*
- *The Visual Edge: Compelling Video Connectors for Your Worship Experience*
- *Mission-Driven Worship: Helping Your Changing Church Celebrate God*
- *An Unstoppable Force: Daring to Become the Church God Had in Mind*
- *A Follower's Life: 12 Group Studies on What It Means to Walk With Jesus*
- *Keeping Your Head Above Water: Refreshing Insights for Church Leadership*
- *Seeing Beyond Church Walls: Action Plans for Touching Your Community*

- *unLearning Church: Just When You Thought You Had Leadership All Figured Out!*
- *Morph!: The Texture of Leadership for Tomorrow's Church*
- *The Quest for Christ: Discipling Today's Young Adults*
- *LeadingIdeas: To-the-Point Training for Christian Leaders*
- *Igniting Passion in Your Church: Becoming Intimate With Christ*
- *What Really Matters: 30 Devotions for Church Leadership Teams*
- *Discovering Your Church's Future Through Dynamic Dialogue*
- *Simply Strategic Stuff: Help for Leaders Drowning in the Details of Running a Church*
- *Preach It!*

With more to follow!

THE
GROWING
LEADER:
healthy essentials
for children's ministry

craig Jutila

Flagship church resources
from Group Publishing

Group resources actually work!

This Group resource helps you focus on "**The 1 Thing**"—a life-changing relationship with Jesus Christ. "The 1 Thing" incorporates our **R.E.A.L.** approach to ministry. It reinforces a growing friendship with Jesus, encourages long-term learning, and results in life transformation, because it's:

Relational
Learner-to-learner interaction enhances learning and builds Christian friendships.

Experiential
What learners experience through discussion and action sticks with them up to 9 times longer than what they simply hear or read.

Applicable
The aim of Christian education is to equip learners to be both hearers and doers of God's Word.

Learner-based
Learners understand and retain more when the learning process takes into consideration how they learn best.

The Growing Leader
Healthy Essentials for Children's Ministry
Copyright © 2004 Craig Jutila

Visit our Web site: **www.grouppublishing.com**

Credits
Creative Development Editor: Mikal Keefer
Chief Creative Officer: Joani Schultz
Copy Editor: Lyndsay E. Gerwing
Art Director: Randy Kady
Designer: Ray Moore
Print Production Artist: Pat Miller
Cover Art Director/Designer: Bambi Eitel
Production Manager: Peggy Naylor

Unless otherwise noted, Scriptures quoted from The Youth Bible, New Century Version, copyright © 1991 by Word Publishing, Dallas, Texas 75039. Used by permission.

Library of Congress Cataloging-in-Publication Data

Jutila, Craig, 1965-
  The growing leader : healthy essentials for children's ministry / by
Craig Jutila.-- 1st American pbk. ed.
      p. cm.
Includes bibliographical references.
  ISBN 0-7644-2620-6 (alk. paper)
  1. Church work with children. 2. Christian leadership. I. Title.
  BV639.C4J875 2003
  259'.22--dc22

                                        2003018176

10 9 8 7 6 5 4 3 2 1   13 12 11 10 09 08 07 06 05 04
Printed in the United States of America.

Contents

Dedication

I would like to dedicate this book to the Children's Staff at Saddleback Church, people I've had the privilege of leading and who have in return led me.

Together we've enjoyed "out of the boxes," "remember when's," birthday parties, summit experiences, retreats, leadership moments, and above all a reliance on God.

You have encouraged, uplifted, and empowered me through your words, actions, and your dedication to the One we serve.

We have rejoiced together and wept together like true family.

Remember to never give up, to fight for the cause, and to stay healthy. Together we will continue to DIVE deeper spiritually. Remember to be responsible for the depth and let God be responsible for the breadth.

It's such a joy to see God work through each one of you on a daily basis. I love serving with you. I love all of you.

Acknowledgments

I would like to dedicate this book to the Children's Staff at Saddleback Church, people I've had the privilege of leading and who have in return led me.

Together we've enjoyed "out of the boxes," "remember when's," birthday parties, summit experiences, retreats, leadership moments, and above all a reliance on God.

You have encouraged, uplifted, and empowered me through your words, actions, and your dedication to the One we serve.

We have rejoiced together and wept together like true family.

Remember to never give up, to fight for the cause, and to stay healthy. Together we will continue to DIVE deeper spiritually. Remember to be responsible for the depth and let God be responsible for the breadth.

It's such a joy to see God work through each one of you on a daily basis. I love serving with you. I love all of you.

Introduction: Ready to Jump In?

We'd driven all the way from California to Del Rio, Texas, and then into Acuña, Mexico. This was my first missionary trip with a group of kids from the church, and I remember rushing around to different churches. I was warmly greeted but didn't know a lick of Spanish. I mean *nada*.

We had arrived late to the first church, and it was already packed. The only pew left was the one in the front row. So, as a visiting pastor, I was taken way up front.

Church was radically different from what I was used to. I decided to pick someone out of the crowd to kind of watch and imitate. *How about the man sitting next to me on the front pew?* He seemed like he knew what he was doing. As everyone sang, the man clapped his hands, so I clapped my hands. When the man stood up to pray, I stood up to pray. When the man sat down, I sat down. When he held the cup and bread for the Lord's Supper, I held the cup and bread.

During the preaching, I didn't understand a thing. I just sat there and tried to look interested—like that man in the front row with me. Then, after the service was over, I assumed the preacher was making some announcements. The people clapped, so I looked over to see if that guy was clapping. He was, so I did too.

Then the preacher said some more words, and I saw the man next to me stand up. Naturally, I went ahead and stood up too.

That's when I heard a few muffled gasps, before a tension-packed hush fell over the entire congregation. I looked around and saw that nobody else was standing. And my previously friendly worship-follower-guy suddenly looked quite concerned (or was it a bit angry?).

I sat down. After the service, the pastor stood at the door, greeting his flock. When I went back to meet him, he said to me in English, "I think you don't speak Spanish."

"Is it that obvious?" I asked.

"I'm afraid so, Señor. You see, at the end of the service I announced that the Acosta family had a newborn baby boy. Then I said, 'Would the proud father please stand up?' "

Have you ever felt that way? You start watching others, standing when they stand, clapping when they clap, reading what they read, buying what they buy, watching what they're doing with their leadership, and kind of follow along? If we're honest, we'll admit that sometimes we really don't know what we're doing when it comes to leading and empowering others. That's why I sat down to write this book.

I've learned a few things from excellent leaders who have encouraged me to put those leadership principles into practice. I want to share what I've learned so you can find ways to apply those proven principles in your ministry, too.

But what theme to use? What "hook" would help you grab hold of those ministry principles?

In considering the early life and development of Jesus—of which Scripture actually says little—I immediately saw the connection to a hobby many people enjoy: scuba diving. (I know, the connection may not be immediately obvious to you, but it made sense to me, OK?)

And I have friends who think there's nothing cooler than jumping off a boat and sinking like a rock into the murky depths.

However, if our ministries are going to be effective (and even enjoyable?), we'll need to clear up any murkiness around four key areas that fit nicely into the acronym "D.I.V.E."—discernment, influence, vulnerability, and exaltation. These are the primary areas in which Jesus himself grew, so wouldn't it be a good idea if we grew in them too? And if Jesus grew up to become the ultimate example of what it means to be a *healthy* leader, then why not follow his lead into healthy leadership in our own ministries?

"Jesus became wiser and grew physically. People liked him, and he pleased God" (Luke 2:52, New Century Version).

Fellow children's worker, all I'm saying is *let's dive down together into the goodness of God.* As we grow in each of these four areas, we will notice him bringing balance into our lives, respect into our relationships, and a greater awareness of our leadership style into our teams. All of this should also result in a clearer focus on the Lord. What could be better?

Yet diving is a dangerous sport. If you don't take the proper precautions, you can get hurt or even lose your life. When you dive in the open water, you must have equipment that sustains life, that propels you, that helps you see clearly, that guarantees a safe return from your underwater adventures.

So I've dedicated each chapter of this book to a piece of essential diving equipment or a crucial diving rule. Together we'll explore the ministry applications of these "Diving Rules and Tools" so we can use them effectively among our church members and within our ministry teams. Each Tool has its special instructions, and each Rule has its theological rationale. If we use a little imagination (not for *interpretation*, but for *application*), we can see that the Bible offers these same tools and rules for a healthy leadership life.

I've found it true in my own life, and I invite you to join me on this D.I.V.E. That's why I've filled this book with lots of down-to-earth leadership advice, mostly learned from my ministry experiences during the past fifteen years of being a children's pastor. You'll find humor here, too, and plenty of real-life stories from my own ministry at Saddleback Community Church in Lake Forest, California. I hope the following twelve chapters will give you the chance to evaluate and grow in your own personal, spiritual walk—all for the good of the children we so dearly love. And if you're studying this book in a small group, I've even included some pointed questions at the end of each chapter to help spark lively discussion.

So...are you ready to dive in and get started?

Craig Jutila
Summer, 2003

Part I: Discernment
(Mental Growth)
Jesus became wiser... (Luke 2:52a)

Chapter 1

All of Us Are Smarter Than One of Us

Discernment recognizes that we're not better off going it alone.

Dive Rule: *Never dive alone.*

This is the First Commandment of scuba diving. You always dive with a partner. A "dive buddy" reminds you to check your air, watch your depth, and stay safe. If something goes wrong, your buddy can save your life.

You've strapped on your tank, adjusted your weight belt, and checked the airflow. You've squeezed the defogger on your mask, zipped up the wet suit, and pulled on your fins. Nothing left but to hurtle down into the murky waters of the ocean. You fall backward off the boat and sink down, down, down until the sun no longer exists for you.

Finally, you reach a silty bottom only to discover, moments later, a rocky outcropping. It feels like an entrance to a cave, and it beckons you to further exploration. You go for it, switching on your trusty Tektite Trek 6000 flashlight as your fins churn the sediment behind you.

You keep moving forward—until the claustrophobia hits. It's a chest pressure that quickly ratchets up, igniting adrenaline bursts of impending panic.

No problem. Just turn around and head back, right?

Wrong. You turn and face a visibility nightmare. The silt has transformed your powerful lamp into a glowworm that illuminates exactly one foot of the soupy mess directly in front of you. Feeling your way by hand, you finally reach the cave entrance and happily chug straight for the surface.

One, two, three powerful thrusts with your fins, and...*ouch!* Your mask digs into the muddy bottom.

Now a big question looms. Its answer will definitely affect your future well-being: *Which way is UP?*

If you're a person who thinks well under extreme circumstances and can stay rational under pressure, then you'll remember a little trick divers use when they experience directional disorientation: Just watch the bubbles.

You see, when you're underwater in low visibility, you can easily lose a sense of which way is up. Deeply submerged, with few visual cues, your senses become overloaded; your mind gets preoccupied. You're in a spot where you could easily make a poor decision, and you know it. Your perceptions narrow. You become disoriented at exactly the moment when you could really benefit from clear thinking.

So experienced divers learn to watch the air bubbles flowing from their regulators. Bubbles float up; follow them, and you can reach the surface.

Experienced divers have another trick that keeps them out of trouble: They only enter the water with their dive buddies. They bring along someone else who can keep an eye on how the dive is going—someone who keeps them out of trouble.

You may be thinking, *OK, Craig, you're going to tell us about healthy leadership, right? What does nearly drowning in the ocean have to do with my keeping our children's ministry on track?*

My point: Ministry leaders need to know which way is up too. And we're subject to the same perceptual narrowing that can cause a diver to panic.

When we're stressed out by the lonely demands of leadership or by the apparent need for rapid-fire decision-making, we become less aware of our surroundings and succumb to a kind of interpersonal claustrophobia. But when we rely on good advice and strong counsel from others, we can pull ourselves out of our narrow thinking. We then can more accurately discern where we are...and which way is up.

This aspect of diving deeper spiritually involves the ability to
· seek wise counsel (because all of us are smarter than one of us), and then
· discern the right direction in decision-making.

The first skill requires humility of mind, the recognition that you need help and can't do it by yourself (all of us are smarter than one of us). The second skill requires a heart compass, or the ability to process information wisely and then make the right decision (head to the surface). Let's look at these two skills a little more closely.

It's Not Just Advice-Seeking

When the Bible talks about the gift of a discerning spirit, it's referring to the God-given ability to distinguish between good and evil. I'm not dealing with that gift in this chapter; rather, I'd like to focus on the idea of obtaining wise counsel and getting good advice no matter what your gifts—so that intelligent leadership decisions can be made by *discerning all the information available.*

I could begin by trying to define exactly what I mean by seeking wise counsel. But since every individual will go about it in unique ways, I'd have some trouble drawing a picture that will hang just right on your own wall. Yet I do know, specifically, some things that it isn't. So consider with me what seeking advice *doesn't* mean...

It doesn't mean seeking everyone's advice. Seeking advice doesn't mean you ask absolutely everyone in your world for his or her opinion and counsel. That would be leadership suicide! Instead, gather a *select group* of people whom you trust, people who have a proven track record and a history of making wise, intelligent decisions.

Not long ago I was doing a conference with a couple of our staff members in Canada. After one workshop, a few people stood around to ask me questions. A young lady who looked about nineteen years old, full of energy, approached me with her pen ready and notebook opened. She asked, "Craig, what makes you successful?"

Huh? Successful? What was she talking about? To be honest, I've never thought of myself as being particularly successful. I'm struggling right along with everyone else. I'm simply doing God's will...I think.

I have, however, considered our team successful. So I thought for a moment and gave my answer: "It's my ability to form a good team."

She was not satisfied with the answer. She followed us all the way into the lobby, into the rain, and almost into the van. I struggled for a fuller explanation, and this is what it was (and this is what I believe): "My success directly correlates with my ability to gather people around me who are smarter than I am." Again, all of us are smarter than one of us. I want to seek guidance, not from everybody but from this special group that knows me, cares for my well-being, and prays with me for God's will to be done.

It doesn't mean getting everybody's _approval_. Seeking advice doesn't mean that everyone will like your decision once you make it. In fact, most of the advice you receive may be conflicting from the very beginning. Someone will say, "I think you should start the new program. Sure, it has a bit of an edge to it, but I think it will be well-received."

You turn to the next person and that person will say, "I think you should hold off starting that new program. The children's ministry has been through several changes this past month, and I think one more will put people over the edge."

Wow. Now what? If you take one person's advice, you know somebody won't like it. Are you OK with that? You'll have to be. Seeking advice doesn't mean seeking approval. Most of the time, you'll receive counsel for and against your ideas. Discerning the right choice is simply a part of the process.

It doesn't mean _avoiding a decision_. For the healthy church leader, "the buck stops here," so to speak. As a leader you will have to make the final decision, the final call. You can't avoid it. Seeking wise counsel and good advice doesn't let you off the hook here. You are simply compiling the information, processing it, and then relaying it. A good leader needs to declare an answer and then live with the consequences of that decision. Wise guidance simply allows the leader to discern the best option, outcome, and solution to the issue at hand. The bottom line, as author Elbert Hubbard once ironically quipped: "To avoid criticism do nothing."

It doesn't mean your decision will be _right_. Question: How can you get in a position to make good choices? Answer: Make some bad choices.

I don't touch hot stoves anymore. Why? Because I touched one before, it hurt, it was hot, and I didn't like the outcome. I don't play hockey without a visor anymore.

Why? Because I've been hit in the face with a stick before, it hurt, it was bloody, and I didn't like the outcome. I don't suck my thumb anymore. Why? Because last week at our children's staff meeting my team said it was immature for me to continue to do it...you get the picture.

The same applies to decision-making. You will make some wrong decisions, but don't give up. You may get hurt, it may be painful, and you may not like the outcome. Great! Learn from your poor decision. File it under "Don't do that again," and move on.

Here is what I know: At some point in your leadership life, you will be in a position to make a similar decision in a similar situation, and you will make the right call. And that, my friend, is called discernment.

Getting Your Decisions R-I-G-H-T

How do we discern the right decision? It usually comes from discerning wise counsel. I have a process in my life that I use whenever a tough (or even easy) decision comes my way. I start with "R" and spell r-i-g-h-t. Note that I end with "T"; I don't start there. I find that many people like to start with the last step in this process, and they end up making poor decisions. I used to start with "T" before I realized the value of others' input and of fully relying on God when choices loomed on my horizon.

But what do the letters stand for, Craig?

I figured you'd ask, so observe the following chart. It shows the acronym's meaning and also offers a powerful Bible verse to back each point.

Can you see how the r-i-g-h-t decisions get made? The process is simple, but implementation is far from easy. So meditate on those verses as often as you can; make them a part of your inner being as you seek good decisions.

And let me comment on a couple key principles I see coming through in this little plan...

First, as you are honing your listening skills, you will definitely want to be ready to learn from the mistakes and successes of others. This is one of the best pieces of counsel you'll ever receive. You don't need to make all of the wrong choices by yourself in order to gain experience. You can observe the action around you. The Bible tells us to learn from the mistakes others make and to learn from the right choices they make as well. Our entire world of relationships is a veritable workshop on decision-making, if we'll only keep our eyes wide open.

I recall once getting ready to go to summer camp. In preparation for camp, Cynthia, one of the ladies on my staff, and I sat down to plan the logistics. During this conversation, she sought my advice. She proposed a new way of signing in our kids before they got on the bus. (We really have to strategize this because we take about four hundred kids to camp and there are ten buses with multiple sign-in locations.) As Cynthia rolled out her new idea to me, I couldn't have disagreed more with what she was saying. The old way worked fine last year, so why change it?

I told her she could do whatever she wanted to do, but I didn't think it would work. The day arrived for check-in, and she had chosen not to take my advice. She

R
equest God's advice. *(Listen to God.)*

"If any of you needs wisdom to know what you should do, you should ask God, and he will give it to you. God is generous to everyone and doesn't find fault with them. When you ask for something, don't have any doubts. A person who has doubts is like a wave that is blown by the wind and tossed by the sea" (James 1:5-6, God's Word Translation).

I
nvestigate God's Word. *(Listen to his Word.)*

"Joshua, be strong and brave! You must lead these people so they can take the land that I promised their fathers I would give them. Be strong and brave. Be sure to obey all the teachings my servant Moses gave you. If you follow them exactly, you will be successful in everything you do. Always remember what is written in the Book of the Teachings. Study it day and night to be sure to obey everything that is written there. If you do this, you will be wise and successful in everything" (Joshua 1:6-8).

G
ather advice from mature experience.
(Listen to your leaders.)

"Obey your spiritual leaders and be willing to do what they say. For their work is to watch over your souls, and God will judge them on how well they do this. Give them reason to report joyfully about you to the Lord and not with sorrow, for then you will suffer for it too" (Hebrews 13:17, *The Living Bible*).

H
ear those you trust. *(Listen to others.)*

"Plans fail without good advice, but they succeed with the advice of many others" (Proverbs 15:22).

T
rust your own experience. *(Listen to ourselves.)*

"The naive believes everything, but the sensible man considers his steps" (Proverbs 14:15, New American Standard Bible).

tried her new way of signing in children—and it worked. I stood there and watched the whole thing proceed flawlessly. In fact, I had at least ten parents come up to me to say how much they appreciated the new way we were doing things.

We would say that Cynthia had discernment. She had observed an inferior method—my old one—and let that be her guide to a better way. (Even though her way put me into counseling for making wrong choices...)

Here's another key principle, related to "hearing those we trust": Repeat advice back to the person who gave it. I have occasionally missed good advice because I hadn't been listening well or I misunderstood what my wise counselor was telling me. Around our children's ministry, it has become part of our culture to respond to advice by saying a few words back to the person who was just talking. We usually pause for a moment and then say these six words: "What I hear you saying is..."

The interesting thing is that most of the time I am wrong! When you clarify the advice someone has given, it puts you in a better position to make wise, intelligent decisions.

Next, as I've said, don't automatically skip to the letter "T" in the process. But here I also want to say that it is *occasionally* OK.

When is it OK? When you find yourself in a situation that is similar to a past experience and you can, therefore, reasonably predict the potential outcome of your decision in the present. That is, throughout your leadership life you will enter certain *déjà vu* experiences—you've "been there, done that." You've had enough leadership experience to gauge a probable outcome to a decision, and so you can give much more weight to the "T"—trusting your own experience.

Finally, in making r-i-g-h-t decisions, you will want to remember two important cautions...

First, beware of reacting rather than responding. This means taking time to process the best words or the best actions in any given situation. Respond; don't just react.

The second caution is to avoid "paralysis of analysis." That is, you can over-react to the idea of not reacting; then you take too much time to respond. In 2002, our Anaheim Angels won the World Series. Before game seven, I went online to check ticket prices. Some tickets were going for $3,000.00 a ticket or more. (A friend of mine sold all four of his tickets for $10,000!) Oddly enough, I went online *after* the deciding game seven, and I found unused tickets for $11.00.

Why did the value of the ticket decrease? Because the window of opportunity had closed. You can buy a ticket now, but why would you want to? You may have to pay a price for good counsel; however, if you wait too long to discern a decision, the value of the wise counsel decreases over time.

Trying to Go It Alone?

"You don't know everything, Craig."

"Why don't you just listen instead of talking all the time?"

"Come on, get somebody to help you!"

Statements from my boss at work? Not-so-subtle advice from my hockey teammates? Or just words of wisdom from my close friends?

No, that's my mom talking. I can still hear such words from my teenage days ringing in my head, years later. Not that Mom was cruel or mean-spirited. She was just plain right.

Sadly, as adults, we occasionally forget that we really don't know it all, and so we talk more than we listen. It's hard to discern good advice when we're always the ones trying to give it. Proverbs 24:6 (New Living Translation) says, "Don't go to war without wise guidance; victory depends on having many counselors." We could also say, "Don't go to teach or lead children without wise guidance; success depends upon having many counselors." Simple paraphrase, once again: *All of us are smarter than one of us.*

But why do some people continue, time after time, to dive alone and refuse the buddy system when it comes to gathering advice? Maybe you've tried it yourself, and you're also asking that perplexing question: *Why?*

Here are four common responses I've heard over the years:

Common Response #1: "I already know it all."

Some people actually believe this. I used to believe this. I never wanted to admit it publicly, but when I got out of college, I did think that I had the world by the tail. I felt I had a pretty good education, made some right choices in college, and just knew that I could roll those decisions over into a productive life of ministry.

Here's what I know, however: It's what you learn *after* you know it all that counts.

"A stubborn fool considers his own way the right one, but a person who listens to advice is wise" (Proverbs 12:15, GWT)

Common Response #2: "I like to take risks."

So do I. But I also know that I need to think through my risks. The idea of "calculated risk" is not an oxymoron; it's the only kind of risk. Seeking the advice and counsel of others puts you in a much better position to make your risked vision a reality.

"Whoever spends time with wise people will become wise. But whoever makes friends with fools will suffer" (Proverbs 13:20, International Children's Bible).

Common Response #3: "I'm usually right on my own."

I must admit that I've actually used this one. And it's true that some people do have a gut instinct—a surprisingly accurate ability to just "feel" what the right decision will be in a complex situation. There are people who believe—and I tend to agree—that those people who seem to have a sixth sense about decisions arrive at those decisions primarily because they've been in a similar situation before. That's why they can closely predict the outcome. In a sense, they've relied on the counsel and experience of others to make a future decision.

However, here is what I know: Arrogance doesn't pounce on you; it seduces you. Through the praise of others and your track record of getting decisions right on your own, you begin to slide into an attitude of arrogance. Soon you're saying, "I don't really need to consult. I will go ahead and make the call on my own." (If you find yourself operating like this, then go directly to Chapter 7 on humility, and do not pass "Go.")

"Pride precedes a disaster, and an arrogant attitude precedes a fall. Better to be humble with lowly people than to share stolen goods with arrogant people" (Proverbs 16:18-19, GWT).

Common Response #4: "I don't have time to get advice."

Listen, you don't have time *not* to. You may end up wasting more time cleaning up from the mistakes you made on your own. Now, I am all for making mistakes. We learn when we make mistakes. As a child, I remember trying to get a bone away from our Australian shepherd, Bonnie.

I approached.
She growled.
I grabbed.
She bit.
I bled.

And I never tried to take another bone from that dog again. I learned from my mistake.

Sure, some situations need quick, on-the-fly decisions, so you make the call and live with the consequences. That's part of leadership. But I'm talking about situations in which you have time to think, strategize, process, and plan. To go without good (and even bad) advice during those times is to waste the intelligence and insight of others. They may hold the missing key to your locked situation. They may be holding the puzzle piece that presents a solution to your problem. Take the time to go after their advice.

"Without leadership a nation will be defeated. But when many people give advice, it will be safe" (Proverbs 11:14, ICB).

Oddly enough, just as I was finishing this chapter, I received a call from our receptionist. She said someone was here to see me, the MOD, which stands for Minister of the Day.

When I walked up to the front, I saw two kids, Amanda and Ben. I call them kids, but one was nineteen years old and the other was twenty-one. As we sat down to talk, the story unfolded:

"Pastor, we feel like we're really in love," said Amanda, "and we're going to get married next month."

"Oh. And how long have you guys been dating?" I asked.

"Well, we've known each other for four months," said Ben. "But we've really only been dating for three. Anyway, Amanda's mom dropped us off here to get some advice before going ahead with our plans."

After an hour of talking with them, I swung around and showed them my computer with the screen displaying my book-chapter notes on how to make a wise decision.

They studied it for a while, and then Ben spoke up with a sly grin, "Huh. Looks like we've only skipped the R, the I, the G, and the H. Not bad!"

Yep. They had gone straight for the "T," totally trusting their own experience.

Now, I know what you're thinking: *They can't be serious.* They have no car, no place to live, no job, no education (and the list could go on). But before you pass judgment on these young people, let me say this—at least they were seeking counsel before making their final decision. Based on our conversation and the information I was able to give them, along with our prayer together, they concluded that they ought to reconsider their decision.

"Oh, the joys of those who do not follow evil men's advice, who do not hang around with sinners, scoffing at the things of God. But they delight in doing everything God wants them to, and day and night are always meditating on his laws and thinking about ways to follow him more closely" (Psalm 1:1-2, *TLB*).

None of us is better off trying to go it alone. We have to look for the bubbles; we have to bring our buddies alongside. It's true in diving, and it's essential in healthy church leadership.

Even Jesus, in his human nature, had to grow in his discernment as he gathered trusted friends to his side. He'd picked up the carpentry business from his father, Joseph. He'd learned the history of Israel from the Word and from the scholars of the day. And surely he was inspired as a preacher from his study of the ancient prophets who came before him. How could we be any less intent upon gathering all we can from the myriad sources of wisdom surrounding us each day?

Dive In! (Questions for Reflection and Discussion)

1. What is your most memorable on-the-water or underwater experience?

2. Have you ever been directionally disoriented? spiritually disoriented? Talk about it!

3. Of the four things that advice-seeking is *not*, which really rings a bell with you? Why?

4. When did you clearly *react* rather than *respond*? What were some of the consequences?

5. When have you seen this principle working well in a practical situation: "All of us are smarter than one of us"? Why is it so easy to forget this principle?

6. Think back through the listening steps in the r-i-g-h-t plan for wise decision-making. In which step are you typically the strongest? the weakest? What one change would you like to make in your usual approach?

DIVING RULES AND TOOLS

Rule: *Never dive alone.*
If there's a First Commandment of scuba diving, it's this: You always dive with a partner. A dive buddy is the person who watches your back. He or she keeps your attention sharp and focused. A dive buddy reminds you to check your air, watch your depth, and stay safe. If something goes wrong, your buddy can save your life.

Spiritual Application:
Don't go solo in leadership. Consult with others. Lead in concert. All of us are smarter than one of us.

Chapter 2

I'm Not Smart, Just Emotionally Intelligent

Discernment includes a willingness to grow in relationship skills.

Dive Tool: *Dive mask*

Because our eyes were designed to see above water, not below it, we need a dive mask. The dive mask puts an air space between your eyes and the water. Now you have a clear underwater view. But how clearly do you view your own strengths, abilities, and weaknesses—and those of others?

I was walking around our children's building just before the 9:45 a.m. service when I noticed several lines of people waiting to get into various classrooms. *What a slow check-in,* I thought. I began talking with the parents in the first line, apologizing for the wait and asking whether they'd consider coming to the 8 a.m. service where the attendance is a bit smaller. Without exception I was told in no uncertain terms that "my child wants to see Mr. Chuck."

I went to the next line, where eight kids patiently stood with their parents. I offered the same option. Again, without exception, the response from each parent went something like this: "I'd go to another service, but my daughter just won't let me do it. She really wants to see Miss Shelly."

What's the appeal? Why would kids *wait in line* to see their leaders?

I have yet to hear a child say, "Miss Becky has a great knowledge of Scripture. My desire is to be in her group today so I can learn the wonders of biblical exegesis." Why? Because kids don't come back for what you teach; they come back, long term, for *who you are.* And who you are is what teaches.

Please understand, it took us three years to encourage our leaders who serve on the weekends (and who once served every other week, or once a month, or twice a year, or only in months that end in "er," or only in leap year...) to serve *every* weekend. Now we have children lining up to see their favorite leaders.

These folks engage the kids emotionally. They lead with passion, energy, and motivation. They share a vision, sure, but they do it in a way that catalyzes change because of their caring, compassion, and empathy. They make a relational, emotional connection.

You see, most leaders bring some skills to the table, but great leaders possess something on top of the usual stuff. It's called "emotional intelligence."

It's All About E.I.

What is emotional intelligence? The term was coined and championed by Dr. John Mayer and Dr. Peter Salovey, along with colleagues like Dr. David Caruso. I appreciate these guys and their pioneering work because I love the notion that I can be smart in ways that don't necessarily show up on my report card.

These men pointed out that we can be smart in our emotions as well as in our rational thinking. We can excel at understanding our own feelings and the feelings of others. We can be intelligent about managing our emotions and the emotions of others. And all that can add up to our being extremely effective, especially when we're working with people.

But we have to know how to use our E.I. Not too long ago, we were having "an opportunity" with one of our sons, Cameron, because he wasn't finishing his lunch before running out to play at recess. Therefore, he was coming home each day with more and more of his lunch not eaten. We kept encouraging him to bring home an empty lunchbox, but eventually we had to go to "Plan B."

Plan B was to write a note to the lunch teacher, letting her know that Cameron was not to be excused until he had at least made an effort to eat his meal. Sure enough, after a few days, the situation improved. However, we created another opportunity with our son, Alec. Alec saw that we were putting notes into Cameron's lunchbox, and he wanted his own note too. (The funny thing was that neither one of our kids could read yet.)

While running late to school one day, Alec asked for his note. We wrote, "Dear lunch teacher, Alec wanted a note in his lunchbox, so here it is. Thanks." Cameron was amazed that the lunch teacher actually knew we were telling him to finish his lunch before he could play, and Alec was happy just to have a note, even though neither one of them knew what the notes actually said.

Emotional intelligence can appear the same way to you and me. We may have a "note," but we really don't know what it says. We have the words but not the meaning.

Digging Deeper: E.I.

How does it compare to IQ?

Most of us know that IQ stands for *intelligence quotient*, and we've all taken tests that measure our IQs. For me, those tests weren't fun because they already proved how intellectually inferior I was to everyone else. I'm the guy who had a cumulative GPA in the low two's in high school, and who crammed four years of college into five years.

Clearly, I'm not a member of Mensa, the society that welcomes people whose IQs are in the top 2 percent of the population. And I'm guessing you may not be a member of that elite, brainy group, either. But here's the great news: There's hope for the other 98 percent of us—*especially* when it comes to growing ourselves into great leaders.

Great leaders know how to work with us, not only through our minds but through our emotions as well. They know how to make us *feel* a compelling vision or *experience* an igniting need in our children's ministry. Great leaders know how to harness our emotions and channel them in the right direction, in stimulating ways. They don't manipulate; they motivate.

Leaders are defined by more than just what they do. They're also defined by *how* they get things done. Here's where we need to look at two kinds of approaches—how resonant leaders accomplish things and how dissonant leaders accomplish things.

Resonant Leaders: They pulsate in tune with others.

The word *resonance* comes from the Latin word *resonare*, meaning "to resound." The *Oxford English Dictionary* says it's "the reinforcement or prolongation of sound by reflection, or...by synchronous vibration."

A piano tuner wants resonant sound; your choir director wants resonant sound. And resonance is equally refreshing in a human relationship. Those who can make it happen possess a valuable skill.

Have you ever been in a resonant relationship in which your spirit felt deeply connected with someone else? You just "felt in synch" with who the person is? Jesus did that in his relationships and in his leadership style.

Jesus obviously resonated with people. He connected with them empathetically—on a feeling level. Take a look at the woman at the well or the woman caught in adultery. Scripture reminds us that Jesus had pity on them, as if they were sheep without a shepherd. Consider the miracles Jesus performed or the glance he gave Peter when this impulsive apostle had denied him three times.

That's emotional connection. That's resonance.

Dissonant Leaders: They sing off key in the group.

In keeping with the music theme, I'll give a dictionary definition of *dissonance* here as "a discordant combination of sounds; lack of agreement or consistency."

Emotionally dissonant leaders are always off key, creating unrelieved tension. Have you noticed these kinds of folks around you? They're everywhere. They convey a harsh, disagreeable combination of sounds; they seem to trumpet discord wherever they go. With dissonant leaders, there's little harmony in team relationships. Anger, fear, and unresolved hurts all typify this leadership style.

It's true; hurt people hurt people. Dissonant leaders are often the proof.

It's critical for leaders to maintain personal and spiritual health. Resonant leaders plan for *margin* in their lives to balance life's load; they have a *mission* for their life's focus; they grow in their spiritual *maturity*; they learn to *manage* their emotions well.

I can remember getting my first job as a children's pastor. Talk about dissonance and someone who was emotionally *unintelligent*—that was me! I told God he had the wrong guy. I didn't do puppets, I didn't do skits, I didn't play the guitar all that well, I couldn't make balloon animals, and I couldn't juggle or do magic tricks. And at the time, I didn't particularly enjoy the presence of children, either.

You see, I wasn't initially *called* into children's ministry...I was *dragged*. Nobody who watched the process could have thought it would last long.

My point: Emotional intelligence competencies can be learned over time, and in the process, you will become a better leader. The reason these competencies can be learned is that they are *spiritual maturity principles that we should be growing in over time.* That's what happened with me.

Before we get to those competencies, let me remind you that it's pretty easy to spot emotional *un*intelligence in others. However, when it comes to perceiving it in ourselves, well, that's another story. Why is this true? Because most of us do not have an accurate picture of ourselves, and that's exactly where emotional intelligence begins.

I recall going with my family to "The Happiest Place on Earth," better known as Disneyland. As we pulled into the parking structure, I spotted the attendant and then immediately turned to my wife to say, "This is going to be interesting."

Why did I say that? The parking attendant's nonverbal cues, her face, her eyes, her body language were all screaming, "Go away!" Sure enough, when I spoke to her pleasantly, she just wouldn't "return the love."

The signs of her emotional *un*intelligence were visible across the parking lot. As I drove off to park the car, I started talking about this lady and how she needed to change her attitude, to be more personable, and to have the right mind-set. I deepened my one-way conversation with my wife by saying that this lady probably didn't have any friends because of the way she treated people.

I mean...
· Who would *want* to be her friend?
· Have you seen the way she *treats* people?
· What kind of facial expression was *that*?
· How *does* she keep her job, anyway?
· ...And so on and so on and yada, yada, yada.

There I was, working myself into a bad attitude by focusing on a lady who had a bad attitude. Can you relate?

My wife reminded me at this point that (a) we were at the happiest place on earth, so I needed to chill out; and (b) somebody may have hurt this lady just a few minutes before, or maybe she was facing a serious crisis at home—there might be any number of reasons for her bad day.

Again, it's easy to recognize emotional *un*intelligence in others. Rarely do we sense it in ourselves. Occasionally, then, it's healthy to look in the mirror, if you know what I mean.

And if you do take a quick peek into the looking glass, will you see E.I. in yourself? It's not too difficult to see because there are some definite signs to look for.

Do You Have It—or Not?

Do you have high emotional intelligence? I'm no psychologist, so please don't consider the questions I'm about to ask you as a definitive test for high emotional intelligence competencies. In other words, the best I can do here is describe some general traits you could expect to see in yourself if God has wired you this way. Then you decide if they describe you.

Personal Competence: Do you manage yourself well?

By "well" I don't mean "perfectly." But is it generally true that you're someone your friends would describe as a good manager of self? In my world, that means I can turn off the hockey game—even when the score is tied!—and take care of what matters even more. Self-management might express itself as...

· *You have self-control.* You can keep your emotions under control as you deal with people. Your impulse to go after the guy in the pickup truck who cut in front of you is something you might think about, but you won't actually do it.

· *You're transparent.* People in your life would describe you as honest and trustworthy. You have integrity.

· *You're flexible.* When situations change, you can change with them to overcome obstacles and take care of business.

· *You're an achiever.* That is, you have a personal standard of excellence, and you manage yourself and your actions to meet that standard.

· *You're optimistic.* When everyone else is upset because the church basement flooded, you're calling up kids and telling them to bring their swimsuits. You see the upside in situations.

· *You show initiative.* You're always ready to jump on an opportunity. *Carpe diem* is a personal motto.

Do these descriptions apply to you? If so, you're probably a good self-manager, and you're more likely to have high emotional intelligence.

Personal Competence: Are you self-aware?

Someone who has high emotional intelligence probably won't find that he's overcome by strong emotions he can't identify. He won't be someone who explodes and can't explain why. Self-awareness shows itself in several ways:

· *You know yourself.* You can identify what you're feeling and how you're affecting others in your world.

· *You have an accurate understanding of yourself.* Both your strengths and your limitations.

· *You're self-confident.* You have a well-grounded sense of your worth and value.

Any of those traits describe you? If not, spend time getting to know yourself better!

Social Competence: Are you socially aware?

People who are highly emotionally intelligent often find that they are aware of how other people feel, what other people need, and what's bothering others. They "read" people well. Social awareness might express itself as...

· *Empathy.* Do you naturally sense what someone else is feeling, and do you communicate that understanding in a warm and respectful way?

· *Political astuteness.* Can you read the road signs nobody else seems to see? Can you predict how your proposal for a computer lab in the children's ministry area will play with the church board—before the meeting?

· *Servant's heart.* Are you someone who sees and meets the needs of your staff, the kids, or others in your world?

Social Competence: Do you possess strong social skills?

Most people, of course, have at least some minimal level of social skills. Without the most basic ability to relate, we just won't "play well with others"—whether we're in the kindergarten sandbox or standing around the office water cooler. But if you have a high emotional intelligence, you may well be a natural "people person" who has success with people in one or more of these roles:

· *Coach*. You're able to give feedback and guidance that increases people's confidence and builds their skills. You constantly provide encouragement and mentoring.

· *Change Initiator*. You're able to bring about change in people and programming. You initiate, manage, and lead in new directions without alienating everyone who's invested in the status quo.

· *Conflict Mediator*. When disagreements arise, you're able to work through the conflicts with the parties involved. You mediate in a way that all parties feel heard, and the issues are often resolved.

· *Empathic Listener*. You listen openly and deeply, and people sense that you understand and feel along with them. You communicate with warmth and respect.

· *Inspirational Leader*. You're able to guide and motivate by communicating a compelling vision in a powerful way.

· *Persuader*. You typically use a wide range of approaches to persuade others. You're a "born salesman." (Hopefully you'll use your persuasive powers for good!)

· *Team Builder*. You easily cultivate and maintain a web of relationships. Plus, you can connect people *with each other* in ways that build collaboration and strong team spirit.

Whew—I don't know anybody who would score perfectly on a test like that. None of us are perfect when it comes to working with other people. But if we want to do effective ministry, we have to grow in our people skills—our emotional intelligence.

But is it worth the effort? Is emotional intelligence really something God wants you to focus on as you grow into a more complete leader?

Is This Stuff Really Biblical?

At this point, you may be wondering: *Is all this talk of E.I. just a lot of secular psychobabble? Is it really relevant for the person seeking to grow in Christ?*

I'd like to address that concern by simply hooking up some key biblical passages with the E.I. points I've been making. So take your favorite Bible version in hand, and come along with me on a whirlwind trip through the Scriptures. I've listed below the E.I. points I made earlier, with passages following the listed E.I. principles and skills.

Personal Competence: Do you manage yourself well?

I. *You have self-control.* You keep disruptive emotions and impulses in check.

"God did not give us a spirit that makes us afraid but a spirit of power and love and self-control" (2 Timothy 1:7).

2. *You're transparent.* You display honesty and integrity; trustworthiness.

"May integrity and honesty protect me, for I put my hope in you" (Psalm 25:21, NLT).

3. *You're flexible.* You're able to adapt to changing situations or overcome obstacles.

"If you wait for perfect conditions, you will never get anything done" (Ecclesiastes 11:4, NLT).

4. *You're an achiever.* You improve performance to meet inner standards of excellence.

"In all the work you are doing, work the best you can. Work as if you were doing it for the Lord, not for people" (Colossians 3:23).

5. *You're optimistic.* You can see the upside in all situations.

"So don't get tired of doing what is good. Don't get discouraged and give up, for we will reap a harvest of blessing at the appropriate time" (Galatians 6:9, NLT).

6. *You show initiative.* You're ready to act and seize opportunities.

"How long will you lie there, you lazy bum? When will you get up from your sleep? 'Just a little sleep, just a little slumber, just a little nap.' Then your poverty will come to you like a drifter, and your need will come to you like a bandit" (Proverbs 6:9-11, GWT).

Personal Competence: Are you self-aware?

1. *You know yourself.* You can read your own emotions and recognize their impact.

"God has made us what we are. In Christ Jesus, God made us new people so that we would do good works. God had planned in advance those good works for us. He had planned for us to live our lives doing them" (Ephesians 2:10, ICB).

2. *You have an accurate understanding of yourself.* You know your strengths, weaknesses, and limits.

"As God's messenger, I give each of you this warning: Be honest in your estimate of yourselves, measuring your value by how much faith God has given you" (Romans 12:3, NLT).

3. *You're self-confident.* You have a sound sense of self-worth and personal capabilities.

"But he told me: 'My kindness is all you need. My power is strongest when you are weak.' So I will brag even more about my weaknesses in order that Christ's power will live in me" (2 Corinthians 12:9, GWT).

Social Competence: Are you socially aware?

1. *You have empathy.* You can sense others' emotions, understand their perspective, and maintain interest in their concerns. You have the ability to feel what others are feeling.

    I once had someone tell me, "I just fake it to make it."

    That is a clear sign of an emotionally *unintelligent* leader. Good leaders don't fake it to make it. They share from their hearts, authentically. They reveal past hurts, concerns, and problems in their lives when situations call for it. They have accurate pictures of themselves and are able to crash through quitting points to connect empathetically with others.

    "When I am with those who are oppressed, I share their oppression so that I might bring them to Christ. Yes, I try to find common ground with everyone so that I might bring them to Christ" (I Corinthians 9:22, NLT).

2. *You're politically astute.* You can read underlying communication currents, along with being aware of the politics within the organization.

    "The naive believes everything, but the sensible man considers his steps" (Proverbs 14:15, NASB).

3. *You have a servant's heart.* You recognize and meet follower, client, or customer needs.

    "Dear children, we must show love through actions that are sincere, not through empty words" (I John 3:18, GWT).

Social Competence: Do you possess strong social skills?

1. *You can coach others.* You bolster others' abilities through feedback and guidance.

    "Let us think about each other and help each other to show love and do good deeds" (Hebrews 10:24).

2. *You're a change initiator.* You're able to initiate change, manage the change process, and lead others in a new direction.

    "Good planning and hard work lead to prosperity, but hasty shortcuts lead to poverty" (Proverbs 21:5, NLT).

3. *You're a conflict mediator.* You're skilled at resolving disagreements.

    "Do your best to live in peace with everyone" (Romans 12:18).

4. *You're an empathic listener.* You listen openly and send convincing messages.

    "My dear brothers, always be willing to listen and slow to speak. Do not become angry easily" (James 1:19, ICB).

5. *You possess inspirational leadership.* You guide and motivate with a compelling vision.

   "Where there is no vision, the people perish: but he that keepeth the law, happy is he" (Proverbs 29:18, King James Version).

6. *You're a persuader.* You can wield a broad range of tactics for persuasion.

   "The wise in heart will be called understanding, and sweetness of speech increases persuasiveness" (Proverbs 16:21, NASB).

7. *You're a team builder.* You cultivate and maintain a web of relationships. You're able to cooperate and collaborate with others while building those skills into the entire team. You can create high morale and team spirit.

   "Therefore encourage one another and build up one another, just as you also are doing" (I Thessalonians 5:11, NASB).

   "Two people are better than one. They get more done by working together. If one person falls, the other can help him up. But it is bad for the person who is alone when he falls. No one is there to help him. If two lie down together, they will be warm. But a person alone will not be warm. An enemy might defeat one person, but two people together can defend themselves. A rope that has three parts wrapped together is hard to break" (Ecclesiastes 4:9-12, ICB).

So the ideas I've shared about emotional intelligence are not without their biblical examples, right? But *knowing about* emotional intelligence and *being* emotionally intelligent are two different things.

The good news: You can grow in this area of life even if it's not your natural bent. You can practice the skills. You can apply the principles. You can get better at connecting with other people in your ministry.

I'll bet you have kids, co-workers, leaders, or volunteers who drain you. I mean, you crawl home from a dinner with the Joneses, and you are *spent.* Your emotional battery has been *drained.* Dinner with the Joneses isn't friendship; it's *ministry!*

On the other hand, my wife and I have some great friends, Oran and Laura. They're like Jesus to us. When we're around them, they always make perfect sense; and they're well-balanced, encouraging, empowering, and uplifting to us.

We all want to be around people like that. Any chance we get, we *try* to be with them. Those people have significant emotional intelligence and use their skills and abilities to connect with and encourage us. But here's something you should know: They probably haven't always been as good at it as they are now. They've grown by practicing the skills and principles.

You Can Make the Connection!

Effective leaders work through other people. But if you can't connect with others in a meaningful, significant way, how will you work through them?

Short answer: You won't. Not until you use your emotional intelligence.

Isn't it true that, when you're ill, you feel better when somebody empathizes with you? If so, you're not alone.

Hospitals that once wouldn't let fathers accompany their wives into the delivery room now almost roll out the red carpet for us dads. We even get official "doctor gear" to wear. We're in charge of the ice chips. And we're the go-to guys when it's time to remind our wives to breathe.

Do you think this is because fathers demanded the right to be where the action was instead of sitting out in a waiting room? Not a chance. It's because years of experience with midwives (and *doulas*, paraprofessionals trained to help women through the birthing process) demonstrated that when a woman giving birth has someone standing beside her and caring for her, things go better. Way better. One study reported that involving a birth doula can reduce cesarean delivery rates by 50 percent and epidural requests by 60 percent. You have to love that!

It pays to invest in relationships in which you give and get understanding, comfort, and empathy. Somehow it not only keeps you happier but also keeps you healthier.

None of this comes as a surprise to Christians. Doctors today are only acknowledging what the Bible proclaimed centuries ago. *Our actions influence others. Our lives intermingle and connect at a deeper level than most of us realize.*

Consider these words from Scripture...

"Happiness makes a person smile, but sadness can break a person's spirit" (Proverbs 15:13).

"Pleasant words are a honeycomb, sweet to the soul and healing to the bones" (Proverbs 16:24, NASB).

As a leader, it's crucial to develop and maintain a healthy emotional intelligence. Constantly ask yourself, "Do I have a cheerful look or a cheerless glance? Do I have a happy heart or a broken spirit?"

I've run into many people serving in ministry who are dead; they just haven't lain down yet. I don't know what you call them in your church, but in our church we call them *deacons*. (Relax; it was just a joke.) Listen, leader: You have a responsibility to the people you lead to be emotionally intelligent in your behavior and actions.

We can look to Jesus for the best example of this. Remember the woman caught in adultery? the people who were hungry? the woman at the well? the leper? I could go on and on. The bottom line: Jesus' teaching was more than just dispensing rational information; he made a relational connection.

I can remember when my sons were four years old and participated in a yearlong drama program at preschool. As the kids sang a closing song at the end of a performance, we parents gave them a standing ovation. We clapped our hands off.

But picture the scene: Onstage, kids were falling down. Kids were out of line. Kids were pulling on their hair, shirts, and pants. Kids were doing weird things with their ears and noses.

Still, all the parents were snapping pictures and applauding wildly. *Bravo!*

I thought to myself, *That was the worst program I've ever seen in my life. Nothing came together, everybody sang off key, kids fell down, kids pouted, and kids even wandered into the audience.*

We gave those budding young stars a standing ovation, not based on their performance but based on the *relationship* we have with them.

That's the same kind of relationship Christ has with us. He loves us based not on our performance but on our relationship, on our simple willingness to be the object of his affection.

So What Will You Do?

Here are two practical things you can do today to connect with people and pump up your emotional intelligence.

Number 1: Smile. Smiles are among the strongest emotional signals you can send. They're almost contagious. Don't believe it? Then try this: Smile at the next ten people you see, especially people you don't know. It's almost impossible for those people to see your smile or look at your countenance and not smile in return.

Number 2: Laugh. Laughter offers a uniquely trustworthy sign of this friendliness. Unlike other emotional signals—especially a smile, which can be feigned—laughter involves highly complex neural systems. It's much harder to fake a laugh than a smile.[1]

In a neurological sense, laughing represents the shortest distance between two people because it instantly interlocks limbic systems. No surprise, then, that people who enjoy each other's company laugh easily and often. Those who distrust or dislike each other laugh little together, if at all. In any work or ministry setting, the sound of laughter is a good gauge of the group's emotional temperature.

Three verses for you to consider:

"A cheerful look brings joy to the heart, and good news gives health to the bones" (Proverbs 15:30, New International Version).

"A happy heart is like good medicine, but a broken spirit drains your strength" (Proverbs 17:22).

"Every day is a terrible day for a miserable person, but a cheerful heart has a continual feast" (Proverbs 15:15, GWT).

Bottom line: Laugh hard and smile a lot. Be an emotional genius.

Dive In! (Questions for Reflection and Discussion)

1. Do you agree that "kids come back for who you are"? When have you seen this principle in action?

2. Are you primarily a resonant or dissonant leader? How can you tell?

3. After answering the E.I. questions, how would you describe yourself? In which specific areas are you the strongest? weakest?

4. Pick two or three of your favorite Bible verses in this chapter. Which one would you like to memorize in the days ahead?

5. What, to you, is the most relevant point about wearing a "dive mask" in children's ministry? What practical steps does it call you to take soon?

DIVING RULES AND TOOLS

Tool: *Dive mask*

Spiritual Application:
See yourself and others more clearly. Remember that to see clearly while diving you need to wear a diving mask. The mask creates an air space to help you see more clearly underwater.

We need a spiritual mask to see our lives through God's Word more clearly. We need to have a clear view of our own strengths, abilities, and weaknesses. We also need to see others more clearly so we can effectively minister to them with a discerning, servant's heart, just as Jesus did.

Notes

1. Meredith Small, "More Than the Best Medicine," Scientific American, August 2000.

Chapter 3

Why Is Common Sense So Uncommon?

Discernment grows when we allow experience and wisdom to combine into common sense.

Dive Rule: *Check your gear before you dive.*

As ministry leaders, we need to check our knowledge and our wisdom. Are they increasing? Are they being nurtured by our commitment to spiritual disciplines?

Just back from vacation. Ready to dig into work again, full steam ahead. But while I was away, I got tired of carrying around so many keys. So I dumped eight of them and determined to make do with a mere three on my ring—car, house, office.

First thing on Monday morning, when I returned to my office after a children's staff meeting, I put my key in the lock and tried to open it.

Nope, it wouldn't budge.

I figured that meant one of two things: Either my boss wanted me to take a much longer vacation (if you know what I mean), or I hadn't put the right key back on the ring. I hoped for the latter explanation.

I went to my assistant Julie's desk, found the duplicate key to my office, and gave it a try. Nope. Didn't turn.

I was beginning to believe the first explanation—a subtle hint that my time "in office" may be drawing to a close. But still hopeful, I checked Crislene's desk for another office key, found it, tried it. Didn't work.

I'm in big trouble now. I put both keys back and took my key out for one last time, praying that it would work. I put it in the lock, nudged it to the left and...nope.

I sat down and, for fifteen minutes, tried to figure it all out. Finally, I just pulled down the handle, and... *Welcome back, Craig! Why didn't you just walk in a half hour ago?*

I had been desperately trying to open an already open door.

On that and many other occasions, I've been forced to look in the mirror and mutter, "How about a little common sense here, Craig?" It's usually after I've done something a little weird, such as...

keeping my garage door open all night;
keeping my car door open all night;
keeping the light on in my car all night;
keeping anything open, on, or running...*all night!*

I've also been known to...
pull on two different socks in the pre-dawn, then make a questionable "fashion
    statement" that afternoon;
mail a letter without stamping it;
stamp a letter without mailing it;
stamp a letter, mail it, then remember I hadn't signed the enclosed check.

More than once I've...
put metal in the microwave;
run out of gas;
made, packed, and then forgotten my lunch;
sent an e-mail to someone who *definitely* shouldn't get it.

And in full public view of too many witnesses I've...
called my own child the wrong name;
called my cat my child's name;
called my dog my wife's name;
called my wife...(you get the idea here).

I'm sure you can't recall any such incidents in your *own* life—times you wished
you could blame someone for what just happened, but you're the only one in sight.

These little mental mistakes don't make a huge impact in our lives, but there *are*
areas of mental growth that make a tremendous difference to both us and our ministries. Our effectiveness as leaders is severely hampered if we don't grow in them.

But first, a bit of review. Here's what we've discovered so far about discernment:
Working together makes us work smarter, and paying attention to and developing
our emotional intelligence makes us more effective with people.

In this chapter, we'll address two areas of mental growth that together increase
our effectiveness and give us what's often called "common sense": knowledge
and wisdom.

In our own lives—and the lives unfolding all around us—we don't automatically
grow in knowledge and wisdom. People don't seem to develop common sense just
because they get older. Why is that? *Why is common sense so uncommon
among us?*

How Do We Get Common Sense?

Toward the end of this chapter, I'm going to offer four practical ways you can
begin leading with common sense. But for now, let me simply say that, to develop
good common sense, we need to get better and better at making use of two God-
given attributes in our lives: *knowledge* and *wisdom.* One does not work without
the other. Alfred, Lord Tennyson said, "Knowledge comes, but wisdom lingers."

The writer of Proverbs said it even better:

"Happy is the person who finds wisdom. And happy is the person who gets
understanding. Wisdom is worth more than silver. It brings more profit than gold"
(Proverbs 3:13-14, ICB).

Knowledge	Wisdom
Knowledge is information.	Wisdom is application.
Knowledge defines our dilemma.	Wisdom discerns a decision.
Knowledge gives us the right direction.	Wisdom helps us follow the right direction
Knowledge detects.	Wisdom discerns.
Knowledge develops our thoughts.	Wisdom deploys our actions.
Knowledge keeps us in the know.	Wisdom helps us grow.
Knowledge gets us the facts.	Wisdom guides our principles.
Knowledge is what we depend on.	Wisdom is what we decide with.
Knowledge is in the head.	Wisdom is in the heart.

In a parable, Jesus told the story of a wise man who built his house on the rock. Why was this smart? Because he built on a firm foundation of knowledge; namely, God's Word. When we make the best choice from among many different alternatives, that's what we call wisdom. It uses knowledge but is more than just knowledge. Observe how wisdom compares and contrasts with knowledge:

Wisdom is having the ability to use knowledge correctly. Understanding (knowledge) helps us make good choices (wisdom). They work best when they travel together.

The great theologian Charles H. Spurgeon once remarked on the difference between wisdom and knowledge. He wrote, "To know is not to be wise. Many men know a great deal, and are all the greater fools for it. There is no fool so great a fool as a knowing fool. But to know how to use knowledge is to have wisdom."[1]

"For the Lord gives wisdom, and from his mouth come knowledge and understanding" (Proverbs 2:6, NIV).

Those words by Spurgeon make me think of my eighth-grade year at Chemawa Middle School. We could choose two elective classes each semester, so I chose wood shop and typing.

I absolutely loved wood shop. I'd walk into that huge warehouse of a class and see all of the cool stuff students and teachers had made—dining room tables, coffee tables, dressers, TV stands, picture frames. These things were unbelievable! I wanted to build some of that stuff too. I knew that, in just a few short weeks, I'd be cranking out furniture as fast as you could say "table saw."

We didn't pick up a single tool for two weeks. Two whole *weeks*, and not a single tool graced my hand. Instead, we went over the safety rules—again and again; we memorized the name of each tool; we observed what each hand tool was designed to do. Then we went over what each power tool was and what it was designed to do. And then we had to take a test (still without the tools).

Still no tools in my hands.

Still no furniture in sight.

A few days later, we talked about plans for our projects. We each received blueprints for making a toolbox. We studied the prints and discussed them—without picking up any tools. We received advice from the teacher on the best tool to use for each particular kind of task. We learned about the qualities of all the various types of wood and which worked best in various situations.

And...still no tools in hand.

Finally, our teacher handed out the wood, and we were about to begin. I couldn't wait to wrap my hands around those tools. The next day he brought a "sample" toolbox that he had made, and it was awesome. Everything precision cut and sanded to perfection. The stain was perfect—no bleeds, no runs—and all the grain was going in the same direction. It was a sight to behold.

And have I mentioned—I really, *really* wanted to grab a tool!

Finally, the day arrived. I had the wood, the plans, the time, and, yes, *the tools.* I knew what to do first, what to do next, and what to do last. I carefully set out on my toolbox-building adventure; and, for the next two weeks, I cut, sanded, glued, and stained.

How exciting to paint the finishing touches on my very own toolbox! I went to the teacher to show him my box. As I entered his work space, I saw that he had his box sitting on the corner of the table.

His box didn't look anything like my box.

His was perfect. Mine was, according to him, a C+.

Why did this happen? I had knowledge. I knew how to make the box. I knew the tools, and I knew what they did. I'd read the plans, cut, glued, sanded, and stained. And after all that...a C+.

I can remember the teacher laughing. Not at me, but at my logic. He was a great teacher, and he said something that has stuck with me because of its simple, powerful insight: "Craig, you have the knowledge to build a great toolbox, but you still don't have the experience or skill."

Experience and skill? Hey, I was thirteen; I wanted a toolbox *now.* Who wanted to take time to accumulate experience and develop skill?

Sorry, but knowledge alone will not build you a great toolbox. Building a great toolbox requires more. It requires the patience that comes with experience, the discipline that comes with skill, and wisdom.

The same is true for all of us, whether we're building toolboxes or ministries. *Knowledge alone does not give us common sense.* That only comes from connecting our knowledge with wisdom.

Luke 2:52a in the New Century Version says, "Jesus became wiser." In the New American Standard Bible, it reads, "Jesus kept increasing in wisdom." According to *Strong's Exhaustive Concordance,* the word *wisdom* in James 1:5 is the Greek word *sophia,* which means "skill" and "wisdom."

Skill and wisdom! Those are what I needed for my toolbox project! To make good choices, navigate life, and develop as a leader requires you to apply what you know to situations at hand. Just knowing stuff isn't enough. Jesus continued to increase in his wisdom; he continued to increase in his ability to apply what he knew.

"If any of you needs wisdom to know what you should do, you should ask God, and he will give it to you. God is generous to everyone and doesn't find fault with them" (James 1:5, GWT).

If you ask for wisdom, God won't just "poof" it to you as if he's using a celestial magic wand. In fact, he may thrust you into a situation—maybe even a painful situation—in which you can gain experience about making wiser, more common sense decisions.

In the Bible, the word most often used for wisdom is *hokmah*, which refers to "skill." *Hokmah* describes the skill of craftsmen, sailors, and other workers. These workers, knowing their trades, also had the skill and wisdom to perform their tasks.

In the spiritual realm, a person who possesses *hokmah* in reference to God is one who is both knowledgeable and experienced in following God's way. In the Bible's wisdom literature, being wise means being *skilled in godly living*. Having God's wisdom means having the ability to cope with life in a God-honoring way. Skill comes from applying the knowledge learned in the classroom, whether a wood shop class or the class of life.

Yet sometimes we just don't apply God's wisdom-gift. We choose to pass by as the Lord reaches out his hand with goodness and guidance for our lives.

We find ourselves on the edge of an opportunity. We clearly have our equipment sitting on the deck right beside us—Bible, prayer journal, devotional books—everything we need to seek God's guidance as we make a ministry decision. But instead of carefully checking our gear before we dive, we throw ourselves into the deep—and pay dearly for our decision.

For instance, suppose a parent comes to you with her child and says, "All the other kids in the class are always picking on little Joey. Can't you make the other kids behave?" How do you respond?

· Do you put an announcement in next Sunday's bulletin, raising your concerns about "discipline problems" in your classes?

· Do you quickly send a note to the parents of all the other kids, asking for better behavior?

· Do you subtly accuse the mother of turning a blind eye to Joey's antisocial tendencies?

· Or do you set up an appointment with Mom and Joey and try to get to the heart of the problem?

Let's face it: Each of us uses *un*common sense every day. And some of the choices we make without involving wisdom can lead to very destructive behavior, damaging ourselves and others.

That's a cost we pay for letting something get in the way of wise behavior.

What keeps us from living in ways that are wise?

See if you've ever uttered any of these three wisdom-blocking excuses...

"I want what I want, and I want it now!"

It's called instant gratification. We want an immediate reward instead of waiting for a better one. We rush into decisions for the immediate pleasure rather than delay our gratification for a later time.

Here's a story that I like from James S. Hewett. Being a Southern California guy, I particularly relate to any story about driving.

A man was sitting in his car at a red light when his car mysteriously died. It just stopped cold. The man looked up and saw that the light had turned green, but in spite of cranking and cranking on the starter, his car's motor wouldn't turn over and catch.

Behind the man, a chorus of honking sounded as a long line of drivers wondered what was holding up forward motion. The worst offender was the enraged driver in the car directly behind the man. The guy leaned on his horn and wouldn't stop.

The man whose car wouldn't start finally got out of his car and walked back to the enraged driver behind him—a dangerous move in today's "road rage" world.

"I'm sorry, but I can't seem to get my car started," said the man. "If you'll go up there and give it a try, I'll stay here and blow your horn for you."[2]

Think about who you are in this story. Are you typically the guy honking the horn or the man who patiently keeps trying to start the car?

The driver was slowly and steadily trying to fix a problem. To the horn-honker, the driver *was* the problem—and the horn-honker wanted the problem solved immediately.

Spiritual growth doesn't come quickly. Wisdom and common sense aren't something you can acquire instantly or buy in the handy gallon size. And you seldom get either if you're so busy wanting something now that you can't wait for a greater reward later.

"I don't want to pay the price of a disciplined life."

It's as if a believer is saying, "I hate paying prices like these, so I'm waiting for a sale." He or she wants to start tomorrow or wait till things look easier or delay until the hectic pace slows down. But it takes work to acquire knowledge and wisdom.

Some folks just aren't willing to pay the price. And make no mistake—the price of following Jesus *is* high. He loves us as we are, but that doesn't mean he doesn't intend to transform us and keep us busy.

One of the key ways we "pay the price" for the kind of growth that Christ's Spirit wants to create within our lives is to be willing to go through hard times. That's right, most every kind of good quality we'll ever develop is the result of a trial or temptation or storm of crisis that we have had to face. We've had to decide how to respond, and then—perhaps much later—we've been able to see how the experience grew within us a more Christlike character.

Here's a practical way to think this through in your own life. Look at the character qualities listed in Galatians 5:22-23a (NIV): "The fruit of the Spirit is love, joy, peace, patience, kindness, goodness, faithfulness, gentleness and self-control."

Anyone who displays these fruits of the Spirit in his or her life has surely paid the price of discipline, right? But make this practical for you! I suggest taking each of these qualities and considering, *What would I likely have to experience in order to develop this quality in my life?* (Note: I've listed a few of my own ideas to get you started.)

Love
(My idea: To become a loving person, I'd probably have to experience what it means to be loved. But I might also need to know—experientially—how painful loneliness or prejudice can be.)

Your idea: _____.

Joy
(My idea: I'd likely know some of the deepest feelings of joy if I'd already had some experience with depression or grief.)

Your idea: _____.

Peace
(My idea: I'd probably value peace the most, and become a person of peace, if I'd learned the devastating results of conflict firsthand.)

Your idea: _____.

Patience
(My idea: I'd likely have to face long periods of tense waiting in order to develop the ability to keep hanging in there.)

Your idea: _____.

Kindness
(My idea: How could I experience kindness from others if I had never been in need? I might have to develop personal vulnerability in order to accept—and convey—kindness.)

Your idea: _____.

Goodness
(My idea: I'd likely have to face evil and know its destructive effects.)

Your idea: _____.

Faithfulness

(My idea: I'd need to know how it feels to have my loyalty significantly tested; perhaps, like Peter, I'd fail a few times.)

Your idea: _____.

Gentleness

(My idea: I'd probably need to be familiar with suffering in order to treat others with compassion and gentleness when they're hurting too.)

Your idea: _____.

Self-control

(My idea: I'd have to be tempted!)

Your idea: _____.

"It's easier to act on what I feel."

All of us tend to act on our feelings instead of doing what we know is God's will.

We have the knowledge to make a wise decision. We may even know the decision we're making is hurtful to ourselves and those around us, that the decision will separate us from friends and family. The decision may cost us financially. Yet we still make that unwise decision and minimize our effectiveness in serving God and others.

I know a man who would probably be considered thoroughly wise by people who know him. His entire life, he has consistently made good choices. He has been raised in church, followed the Lord's leading, and even served in ministry.

But his effectiveness will soon end because of an unwise decision. With a wife and year-old baby at home, he says he's in love with another woman.

People have talked to him, reasoned with him, and tried to give him insight and knowledge into what he's doing to himself and his family. They've gone to him—not screaming, yelling, or pointing fingers, but as concerned friends and family members. When the issues are laid out before him and the consequences clearly defined, grief and pain show in his eyes.

Yet as the questions unfold, his heart shuts down...

"Do you know that what you're doing is wrong?"

"Yes."

"Do you realize the poor choice you are making?"

"Yes."

"Do you acknowledge the negative impact this will have on your family and friends, people who truly love you?"

"Yes."

"Do you understand that this will tarnish your testimony and hinder your service in the Kingdom?"

"Yes. But..."

Sadly, that "but" shuts down all progress in connecting what this man knows with wisdom. He's not using his knowledge well. He's not being wise. Knowledge without wisdom is useless.

Consider what we find in the book of Isaiah:

"You felt secure in all your wickedness. 'No one sees me,' you said. Your 'wisdom' and 'knowledge' have caused you to turn away from me and claim, 'I am self-sufficient and not accountable to anyone!' So disaster will overtake you suddenly, and you won't be able to charm it away. Calamity will fall upon you, and you won't be able to buy your way out. A catastrophe will arise so fast that you won't know what hit you" (Isaiah 47:10-11, NLT).

There is a selfish knowledge and an ungodly mind-set that does not sink its roots into God's Word but rather into our own fickle hearts. We begin to esteem what we feel more highly than what we know God says.

The word for that self-serving view of life? *Rationalization*. We can rationalize anything. But in order to have a firm foundation, we need knowledge of God's Word that leads us to solid, common-sense wisdom.

Whether it's living your life as a spouse, an employee, or a ministry leader, decide that you want to know God and his Word, to apply what you know to your daily situations, and to live in wisdom. That's God's heart for you.

Consider these words from James:

"If you are wise and understand God's ways, live a life of steady goodness so that only good deeds will pour forth. And if you don't brag about the good you do, then you will be truly wise. But if you are bitterly jealous and there is selfish ambition in your hearts, don't brag about being wise. That is the worst kind of lie. For jealousy and selfishness are not God's kind of wisdom. Such things are earthly, unspiritual, and motivated by the Devil" (James 3:13-15, NLT).

L.E.A.D. With Uncommon Wisdom!

If you want common sense—a ministry-enhancing, discipleship-enabling blend of knowledge and wisdom—the chart on page 42 provides four ways to go about getting it.

This week be intentional about shifting the focus of your heart and mind to seek *God's* heart and mind. That's where true wisdom lives.

Let's check our gear before we dive. It's only common sense to do that!

L
isten to the experience of others.

There are people around you whose godly common sense you respect. Hang out with them. Ask their advice. Engage them as mentors. Soak up insight from these people.

And don't delay; seeking wisdom is hugely important! Consider these words from Proverbs:

"Getting wisdom is the most important thing you can do! And whatever else you do, get good judgment" (Proverbs 4:7, NLT).

E
xplore God's Word.

Yeah, you read the Bible so you can prepare ministry messages...but do you read it for you? Do you let the two-edged sword slice away your apathy or worry? Is the Bible impacting your life?

"Wisdom begins with respect for the Lord. And understanding begins with knowing God, the Holy One" (Proverbs 9:10, ICB).

A
pply God's wisdom.

Remember, it's not just what you know; it's what you do. Knowledge that doesn't inform your attitudes and actions is useless. God isn't all that impressed with your dazzling command of Bible trivia; he's impressed with your heart and how you're serving him in the world.

"This is what we are proud of, and I can say with all my heart that it is true: In all the things we have done in the world, we have done everything with an honest and pure heart from God. And this is even more true in what we have done with you. We did this by God's grace, not by the kind of wisdom the world has" (2 Corinthians 1:12, ICB).

D
evelop a disciplined life.

Do you balance your life, investing in your leadership, family, job, and church in appropriate ways? Do you fast? Do you give? Do you have accountability and authority in your life?

It's your job to make that all happen. You're the disciple.

"My child, hold on to wisdom and reason. Don't let them out of your sight! They will give you life. Like a necklace, they will beautify your life. Then you will go on your way in safety. And you will not get hurt" (Proverbs 3:21-23, ICB).

"But if any of you needs wisdom, you should ask God for it. God is generous. He enjoys giving to all people, so God will give you wisdom" (James 1:5, ICB).

Dive In! (Questions for Reflection and Discussion)

I. Recall my list of things I did that showed a lack of common sense (keeping the garage door open, keeping the car door open...). Which have you done yourself at some time? What actions of your own could you add to the list?

2. In what ways do you view yourself as a wise person? as an unwise person?

3. Who is the wisest person you have known in your lifetime? Think through some of the qualities you admire in this person. Which of those qualities would you like to emulate?

4. What does it mean to you, personally, to become "skilled in godly living"? Name a recent success in this endeavor.

5. When in your life have you made an unwise choice? Did you "know better"? If so, what kept you from letting your knowledge guide your choice?

6. What is your answer to the question "Why is common sense so uncommon?" What is your solution to this problem when it comes to your ministry efforts?

DIVING RULES AND TOOLS

Rule: *Check your gear before you dive.*

Spiritual Application:
You have your dive equipment strapped on, and you're ready to go. You slide over the edge of the boat and feel the cool water surround you.

That's when you take your first breath through your gear and suck in a lung full of...*nothing*. The gauge on your gear tells you there's plenty of air available, but none of it is getting to you—and you're underwater. What could be wrong?

The answer: Your regulator is broken, and now you're in trouble.

Common sense would have suggested you take the first breath of air from your tank through your regulator *before* plunging off the boat. You'd have known that the regulator wasn't working before you depended on it.

But now you're six feet under water and your dive is over as you reach for the surface.

We know we should test our equipment, but we sometimes choose to rush into the dive instead. We want to get below the water; we want to hurry up and have fun. We don't want to take time to do all the smart things we know we should do to guarantee we're ready.

As one ministry leader to another, let me ask: How is your "regulator"? Is what you know about God and his ways informing your decisions? Are you sure your "tank" is full and you're spiritually prepared to do ministry? Are you being nurtured by your commitment to spiritual disciplines? If so, you'll breathe heavenly life into yourself and become a "breath of fresh air" to all who follow you.

Notes
1. Quote by Charles Spurgeon found at this Web site: http://www.brainyquote.com/quotes/quotes/c/ql21393.html

2. Adapted from James S. Hewlett, ed., *Illustrations Unlimited* (Wheaton, IL: Tyndale House Publishers, Inc., 1988).

Part II: Influence
(Physical Growth)
...and grew physically. (Luke 2:52b)

Chapter 4

Leading From the Inside Out

To use our influence well, we must see ourselves and our leader-ship as we are—and choose to make changes.

Dive Tool: *Dive computer*

It's worth the effort to stop occasionally and check our internal dive computer. At some point we all reach crush depth, when a little self-leadership would have helped us return to the surface safely.

Ron looked over at me, pointed at a golfer on the next green, and said, "He plays the ball down." I'd never heard the term, though I'd been golfing for many years. (I know, I'm switching sports here, but bear with me, please. We'll get back into the water soon enough.)

"What do you mean by 'playing it down,' Ron?" I asked. "Don't we all play the ball down? I mean, the only time it's in the air is when we hit a shot. But every time it goes up, it comes down again, right?"

"Not what I mean, Craig. See, this guy plays the ball all the way into the hole."

"Well, I play the ball all the way into the hole as well."

Ron grinned then and asked, "You mean to tell me, Craig, that you never accept a 'gimme'?"

In case you don't know, in the game of golf, if you're close enough to the hole on the green, one of the other players will often say, "I'll give you that one." Then you don't have to putt; you can simply pick up the ball. In other words, you don't play the ball "down" into the cup.

Ron also asked me if I'd ever taken a "mulligan." A mulligan is a substitute shot if your first one is bad. If, for example, you tee off and wildly slice your ball into a nice, shiny Lexus sitting in the parking lot, you simply take a mulligan—a "do over"—instead of taking the required two-stroke penalty (and finding out who owns that fine car!).

I had to start thinking long and hard about my golf scores. Sure, I'd pick the ball up when somebody gave me the putt. I would also take a mulligan or two each round, and I would even "improve" the ball's position in the fairway to get a better shot. In fact, as I thought about it, I realized that Ron and I never consistently played the ball down. We were mulligan-happy, and we often gave each other close putts.

So Ron and I had a little meeting. We decided that we would play the ball down from that day on. We were going to play it as it sat, count every stroke, allow no gimmes, and take every penalty stroke according to the rules of the game.

It actually felt better. No little lies, no bending the rules, no fooling ourselves as to what we really shot at the end of the day.

There's a simple point here for all of us in leadership who wrestle with self-leadership issues: You cannot clean up your external game until you start doing some appropriate internal things because *all leadership starts from within*. Sure, you can bend the rules, even break some of them. But if you continue shortcutting your integrity, you will never have peace.

Ron and I bought new equipment, played more, studied the game more, and played the ball down. Yes, our scores changed—they went much higher! However, each time we walk off the course, we feel good about being honest and above board. Any leader who approaches life with this attitude is better off for it.

In this chapter, I'd like to look closely at what it means to lead from the inside out. You cannot fake it to make it in this business of self-leadership. You are either doing appropriate self-leadership or you aren't. You're either demonstrating discernment or you aren't.

I think the Apostle Paul nailed it when he was teaching Timothy to be a healthy leader. Check it out: Paul spent more time talking about Timothy's character, role, and responsibility than about the "work" Timothy was doing. What does that say about self-leadership?

Paul was always zinging Timothy with little reminders like this:

"Keep a close watch on yourself and on your teaching. Stay true to what is right" (I Timothy 4:16a, NLT).

What does it take to lead from the inside out and play the ball down in church ministry? I've boiled it down to the three R's—Ruts, Reminders, and Rhythms. A good leader knows how to handle internal ruts. He or she develops a set of powerful reminders that keep him or her fired up for ministry. And good leaders have a rhythm of leadership that lets them quickly recognize when things are out of kilter in their lives. So...ready for the Three R's of self-leadership?

As you grow in them, you grow in influence.

Ruts: Getting Stuck in the Seamy Side of Self

We all slowly create ruts in our lives. We get stuck in certain routines, and we just expect things to unfold before us as they've always unfolded. Then, if something changes or unusual problems arise, we panic and become moody, irritable, raging, and generally hard to live with. This works to destroy our credibility with those we seek to lead.

Here's a (probably untrue) story I like along these lines, showing just the opposite reaction. It seems the great violinist Nicoló Paganini was performing in Italy, center stage, backed by an entire orchestra. As the spotlight gleamed off his antique violin, the unthinkable happened—a string snapped.

Without missing a stroke, the virtuoso continued, adjusting, playing the difficult classical piece on the remaining three strings. The audience watched in amazement as Paganini flawlessly flashed through the next few bars of music.

Then an amazed gasp arose throughout the concert hall as a second string snapped. Now two strings hung down, and again Paganini seemed unfazed as he played on. Still the music poured out of the violin and washed across the crowd.

Then—you guessed it—another string snapped. The audience was scarcely breathing as the violinist completed the final few bars of music, perfectly, with just one string.

The audience exploded to its feet, rocking the house with thunderous applause. On the stage, Paganini stood as if in a daze. He'd created more music from one string than most violinists could have coaxed out of four.

This story is about talent, but it's also about self-leadership under pressure. It's about Paganini discerning the goal and exerting self-leadership to overcome an unexpected obstacle. He proceeded in confidence.

I think self-leadership ruts are simply areas in our lives in which we get stuck in our own assumptions and selfishness. I've listed a few potential ruts below, some of which may typically tempt you more than others. Look at the list and see if you can find your sticking points by making a check mark next to the appropriate letter. (Note: If you are studying this book in a group, be ready to talk about *why* you marked the letters you chose.)

Which Ruts Are Your Personal Favorites?
I. Bad attitude. When it comes to my normal frame of mind, it's...
___ A. "Everybody watch out! I have now entered the building."
___ B. "My only desire is to please you in every way, ladies and gentlemen."
___ C. "I just naturally assume the best about people and situations."
___ D. Other (explain): _____.

2. Arrogance. When it comes to knowing my abilities, it's...
___ A. "I'm pretty good at some things; I leave the rest to those who do it better."
___ B. "I feel like I can learn something new from just about anybody."
___ C. "It's my way or the highway, Buster."
___ D. Other (explain): _____.

3. Lack of purpose. When it comes to knowing *why* I'm where I am, it's...
___ A. "This is just a temporary stop along the way. What I *really* want to do someday is..."
___ B. "I know God has put me here to accomplish a purpose. I'm going to bloom where I'm planted."
___ C. "Everything always seems so disorganized around here. Most days it seems pointless to even try."
___ D. Other (explain): _____.

4. Laziness. When it comes to getting things done, it's...
___ A. "Hey, why do today what I can put off until tomorrow?"
___ B. "Take up the slack? I thought you said, 'Hit the sack.'"

___ C. "By constantly looking ahead, I've been able to plan everything more efficiently and get more done."

___ D. Other (explain): _____.

5. Busyness. When it comes to getting things done, it's...

___ A. "Son, you shouldn't be sitting there playing games. After all, you're four years old now—time to *produce!*"

___ B. "I've burned the candle at both ends for so long that I'm drowning in wax!"

___ C. "Better to rust out than burn out. Relax!"

___ D. Other (explain): _____.

6. Unresolved anger. When it comes to what's bothering me, it's...

___ A. "I usually speak directly and assertively about what's bugging me."

___ B. "I prefer to 'go postal'; it solves everything in one blazing moment of devastation."

___ C. "It's called passive-aggressive behavior; deal with it! (Or not, OK?)"

___ D. Other (explain): _____.

7. Moodiness. When it comes to my emotions, it's...

___ A. "We're talking roller coaster here. Welcome to the wonderful, topsy-turvy world of my changing disposition."

___ B. "Stiff upper lip, old boy. That's me."

___ C. "Oh, no! What rotten timing! I'm just going to die! A *pimple!*"

___ D. Other (explain): _____.

8. Hurt. When it comes to dealing with conflict, it's...

___ A. "You hurt me. I'm definitely going to hurt you back."

___ B. "Sarcasm usually works best for me—or just pretending I never felt a thing."

___ C. "I keep having these terrible headaches. (Yes, everything's just fine at the church, Doc.)"

___ D. Other (explain): _____.

Anything look familiar? Hey, if they don't, maybe you could read this list to your staff or a few close friends. I'm willing to bet they'd help you identify one or two ruts you've fallen into without realizing it.

Remember, when you're growing in influence, you're growing in your ability to apply what you know and leverage it to lead others. That means you have to know stuff, including stuff about yourself. When you discover something true about yourself and your leadership style, that gives you the opportunity to choose to let God deal with you. And that, my friends, is wisdom.

On the evening of August 3, 1992, eight men lined up for the first semifinal of the 400-meter race at the Olympic Games in Barcelona. And I was there. (Not there in Spain, of course. I was there in front of my television set.) What happened in that race will stay with me as powerfully as if I'd been one of the 65,000 fans filling the Olympic Stadium.

Derek Redmond, a British runner and a medal contender, burst out of the blocks as if he'd been shot out of a rifle. All the years of training and all the races he'd run to prepare him for this moment were carrying him toward his goal—the finish line.

Then Redmond's hamstring muscle ripped, and, 250 meters from the finish, he collapsed onto the track.

Moments passed as he grimaced in pain. Then, slowly, Redmond got up and hobbled along the track, limping for the finish line.

The other runners were long gone. The race was finished, but not for Redmond. And not for someone who loved him. With 100 meters left to travel, Redmond's father ran from the stands and put his arm around his son's shoulders. And in what has become a symbol of the Olympic ideals of perseverance and determination, the two men slowly finished the race—together.

Derek Redmond didn't win a medal that day, but he finished the race a winner. When everyone in the stadium thought he would give up, Redmond continued with determination. He persevered.

Can you persevere in daily attempts to get unstuck, to move out of the ruts that plague you? If so, you'll enjoy a profound new effectiveness in ministry and in all your relationships.

Tape up these wise words from Paul over your desk:

"Don't get discouraged and give up, for we will reap a harvest of blessing at the appropriate time" (Galatians 6:9b, NLT).

If you're stuck in a leadership activity or style that's not working—or not honoring God—you can crawl up and out of that rut. What's required is insight, a desire to change as you rely on God, and perseverance.

And what helps us with perseverance? *Reminders!*

Reminders: Burning Hot for Him

We all need some reminders that accentuate our routines. I'm always saying, "Let's get fired up." Well, here is the million-dollar question: *Who or what fires you up?*

For me, it's certain experiences, stories, and visual reminders—things that light my ministry fires with energy and enthusiasm for Kingdom work.

They remind me why I am here.

They remind me of my calling.

They remind me to keep growing as a leader.

Reminders are the key to keeping my fires burning hot for Christ. For example, I can't walk into my office without getting excited. Just looking around the room gets me fired up! My eyes immediately fall upon a mug (I'll tell you about this mug later), a picture, a drumstick, and a mirror. They're reminders of a history in ministry that encourage me in the present and keep me looking into the future.

Watching volunteers give 100 percent and serve with their God-given gifts fires me up. Green lanyards fire me up because leaders who have served five years in our children's ministry wear green lanyards instead of blue ones on their name tags. Lines outside of classrooms fire me up. Talking with and helping other churches and hearing what God is doing among their people fires me up.

What are nine or ten things that fire you up and keep you going? What experiences, stories, and visual reminders keep you passionate because they bring you back to your purpose in ministry? As you generate your personal list, keep these three pointers in mind:

First, *keep going back to experiences that fill you up.*

These special occasions, rituals, and events remind us of who we are in the Kingdom, where we've been, and where we're going. They include such things as baptisms, communion, retreats, prayer practices, art, music, poetry—anything that nurtures your spirit.

Second, *cling to stories that fire you up.*

They're meaningful illustrations that touch your emotions and remind you of what you want to accomplish.

Here's a story that does it for me. It has to do with "Superman"—Christopher Reeve. He was born September 25, 1952, in New York City. Christopher Reeve loved the horse-related sport called *eventing* which combined the precision of dressage with the excitement of cross-country and show jumping.

In May of 1995, during the cross-country portion of such an event in Culpeper County, Virginia, Reeve's thoroughbred, Eastern Express, balked at a rail jump, pitching his rider forward. Reeve's hands were tangled in the horse's bridle and he landed head first, fracturing the uppermost vertebrae in his spine. Reeve was instantly paralyzed from the neck down and unable to breathe. Prompt medical attention saved his life.

This most self-reliant and active of men was now facing life almost completely immobilized and dependent on others for his most basic needs.

Reeve said, "This accident has been difficult for all of us. But it hasn't frightened anybody away...We all miss the activities...I'd be kidding you if I said I didn't miss that. Ultimately, you have to accept that *being* together is more important than *doing* together."[1]

One thing we know for sure: Christopher Reeve did not lose his attitude or his self-leadership. He has shown the world his attitude of perseverance and his will to continue. This is a story that gives me a new grip, strengthens my soul, and keeps me fired up.

Third: *Create visual, physical memories that free you up.* These are usually external objects that remind you of the reasons you're doing what you're doing.

With visual reminders around us, we can constantly rediscover: "Hey, that's what we're all about! That's why we are all here!" We get fired up about it all over again.

At my church we have three signs on one of our walls. The first sign says, "Belief." Basically, with God all things are possible. We know it can happen. The second sign says, "Grow." The third says, "Teamwork."

Those signs remind us of the things we value, and seeing the words daily acts as a constant reminder for our staff to remember, "Here's what we're all about." Let me give you some examples from my own life...

When I speak at children's ministry conferences, I'll often bring with me a little bag of "reminder goodies" to use as examples. I usually bring along a little mug that displays the smiling faces of sixth-grade kids on it. On the back it says, "We love you, Craig." Isn't that sweet?

I received that cup from the very first small group we started for children, called Ten for Ten. Our goal was to gather ten kids and, for ten months, meet with them and teach them some spiritual things, then take them on a mission trip where they could live out some life application. We put these kids in a van in California and drove all the way to Texas.

The mug is now ten years old, but I remember these young ladies. One of them, Natalie, is now on my staff at Saddleback in our children's department, and the others are also moving ahead to do great things in their lives. The little mug stays on my desk and helps me remember, "Craig, you had something to do with their spiritual growth. That is treasure in heaven." It serves as an empowering moment in my life that keeps me passionate about the present. That mug represented ten; we now have over 1,300 kids in small groups.

I also bring along something else I keep in my office—a little statue of a wolf in sheep's clothing. It's important to me, and here's why: When we wised up and stopped driving to Texas, we started flying. We went from ten to over thirty sixth-graders on a plane (and it's *amazing* how fast adults will relocate themselves on a plane when you walk onboard with thirty kids). We would take children on a mission trip to Mexico and then fly back. After one particular trip, I was absolutely exhausted.

I remember being on a flight home from San Antonio, and the kids were quiet—a perfect time to take a nap. I'd been asleep only a couple of minutes when I awoke to hear my name over the loudspeaker. I looked up, and there were five of our kids at the front of the plane making an announcement. On the PA system. I thought, *What's going on? They've lost it!*

The kids were thanking my wife and me, presenting us with that little statue. I keep the statue on my desk so I can look back at our groups and the kids we minister to and think, *This is why we do what we do—because we're making an impact.*

I once took our staff members on a retreat to Palm Springs. During one of my teaching sessions, they stopped the meeting and spent the next hour passing around a baseball jersey. Each one of them had written an adjective on the jersey that they felt best described my leadership, along with an associated verse. Talk about an empowering moment!

I'll never forget what they said. The jersey has a permanent place in my office, and when I get discouraged, when I feel a bit inadequate in my role, when I feel like throwing in the towel, I look at that jersey and say, "No way, baby. I am in this for the *long* haul!"

What physical reminders could you place around you? What do you need to look at regularly to fire up your passion? to remind you of God's work in your past, his presence within you today, his plans for your future?

Don't ignore this technique, for it's a way God has chosen to work with us humans. In the Old Testament, when the army crossed the Jordan River to conquer the Promised Land, men set up stones on the far side so all who saw (especially the children) could recall the great things God had done.

Often I have to walk right up to "quitting points" because I have to get up close to them in order to crash through them. The jersey on my wall, the picture of my staff on the roller coaster at Disneyland, a pencil that says, "Made on Purpose," a baseball bat from our first conference, pictures of kids in the baptismal pool, letters from parents, letters from kids, letters from leaders. Those simple physical objects are powerful reminders of the reason I need to discern my purpose and stay the course.

Then there's the crown of thorns from Jerusalem—the reminder that Christ didn't give up. People mocked him, and he didn't give up. People made fun of him, and he didn't give up. He was nailed to a cross, and he didn't give up.

So I don't have to give up, either.

Yet we are tempted, tempted, *tempted* to give up! To lose sight of why we're in this sometimes difficult and amazing thing called ministry.

So along with external reminders I can put in my office, I cultivate internal reminders—basic truths that I recall when I'm under pressure. Let me share with you three of the most crucial internal reminders that carry me through, that help me lead from the inside out.

I. People will let me down.
Reminder: Sustain the strain!
Who was let down by people more than Jesus?

"He went to his own people, and his own people didn't accept him" (John 1:11, GWT).

But Jesus focused on his purpose—the redemption of mankind—and he went to the cross, paid the price, and redeemed mankind.

Does practicing self-leadership cost us anything? Absolutely. It cost Jesus his life. It will cost us our humility, consistency, resiliency, and tenacity. This was the kind of "sustaining the strain" that challenged the original disciples and challenges us, too.

Take a look at Matthew's description of Jesus' self-leadership and commitment to his purpose, God's plan, and our good:

"He took Peter and Zebedee's two sons with him. He was beginning to feel deep anguish. Then he said to them, 'My anguish is so great that I feel as if I'm dying. Wait here, and stay awake with me.'

"After walking a little farther, he quickly bowed with his face to the ground and prayed, 'Father, if it's possible, let this cup of suffering be taken away from me. But let your will be done rather than mine.'

"When he went back to the disciples, he found them asleep. He said to Peter, 'Couldn't you stay awake with me for one hour?' " (Matthew 26:37-40, GWT).

And consider these additional examples of Jesus' self-leadership...

· Fasting for forty days. (He could have given up for the devil.)

· Telling Judas to go and do what he needed to do. (He could have halted the betrayal.)

· Being arrested. (He could have escaped; he'd done it before.)

· Going to the cross. (He could have called angels down to rescue him.)

In spite of Jesus' awesome example for me, sometimes my own self-leadership tank is empty. I don't do the appropriate things to keep myself moving and motivated. My quiet time and Scripture memory take a second place to my "to-do" list. I begin to complain, and my bad attitude begins to affect those around me in a negative fashion.

So I've put together a little mental exercise that snaps me back into a healthy, disciplined, self-leadership mind-set. Try it for yourself. Quote these few lines, and you'll regain a proper perspective. You'll feel your self-leadership attitude coming back in line.

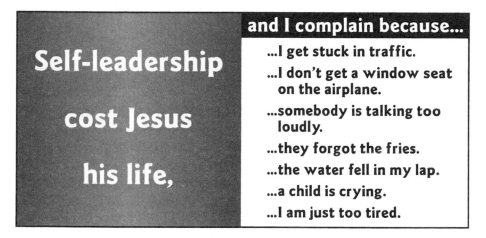

Self-leadership cost Jesus his life,

and I complain because...

...I get stuck in traffic.

...I don't get a window seat on the airplane.

...somebody is talking too loudly.

...they forgot the fries.

...the water fell in my lap.

...a child is crying.

...I am just too tired.

2. Problems make me focus on today.
Reminder: Focus on the future!

In the book *A Savior for All Seasons*, William Barker relates the story of a bishop who once visited the home of a college president who lived in the Midwest. The president also served as a physics and chemistry professor at the college.

The bishop sat back after dinner one evening and announced that as far as he was concerned, it was about time for the millennium to arrive. After all, nature had been thoroughly explored, and everything that could be invented had been invented. People were even driving horseless buggies!

The college president politely raised a hand and disagreed. Certainly there would be more inventions and discoveries.

The bishop huffed—he wasn't accustomed to being challenged. He insisted that his host name one possible invention that hadn't already been conceived. The president thought a moment and made his prediction: Within fifty years someone would invent a device that would let people fly.

The bishop was offended. Certainly only angels were meant to fly! Bishop Wright went home later, where he undoubtedly hugged his two sons, Orville and Wilbur...who in a few short years accomplished what their father thought impossible.[2]

Who knows what tomorrow may bring? If we dwell only on the problems of the moment, we squelch our vision of future possibilities. When you're leading from the inside out, you see your world with a sort of "double vision"; you recognize the challenges in front of you that you have to handle. But you also look at your life and ministry through the focus of faith—knowing God can do remarkable things.

"All of these things are for your benefit. And as God's grace brings more and more people to Christ, there will be great thanksgiving, and God will receive more and more glory.

"That is why we never give up. Though our bodies are dying, our spirits are being renewed every day. For our present troubles are quite small and won't last very long. Yet they produce for us an immeasurably great glory that will last forever! So we don't look at the troubles we can see right now; rather, we look forward to what we have not yet seen. For the troubles we see will soon be over, but the joys to come will last forever" (2 Corinthians 4:15-18, NLT).

Let's look at our problems, not merely in light of the *future* but in light of *eternity*.

3. Discouragement will drain me.
Reminder: Persecution leads to promise!

Each of us sees the world through a set of lenses called *values*, and our behavior as leaders is driven by these values. Our world is colored by these values, and we often act in accordance with them. What do your values say about discouragement? It is important for you as a leader to find a way to fight the discouragement that can hinder us.

We can become discouraged when a program bombs. When a parent complains. When it seems no matter what we do, it's never enough.

We may not be able to change how people treat us, but we can exert self-leadership and determine how we'll respond.

I know a guy who, at family functions, will often just walk out without letting anyone know where he's going. Most of the time, no one misses him. However, if someone asks about his presence, the typical response is "Oh, he left for a few minutes to take a drive; he'll be back shortly."

When I asked him about this behavior, he told me that he just needs a break, some time alone. He says that everybody knows this is just "who he is."

But what he does is simply rude. And the behavior stems from some internal value that drives this selfish behavior. Yes, he's probably drained. Yes, he may be discouraged. But he's choosing how to respond. He has the ability to choose another behavior.

If we don't apply some self-leadership in our lives, we'll likely become discouraged in our ministries at some point. When you lead, you attract your share of criticism and "constructive criticism," and both can be debilitating. When it comes to discouragement, especially discouragement in response to unjust persecution, we *must* focus on the big picture of what God is trying to accomplish through us and our ministries. The Apostle Paul had the right idea: to stand firm in the face of discouragement by focusing on God's eternal promises.

"Join with others in following my example, brothers, and take note of those who live according to the pattern we gave you. For, as I have often told you before and now say again even with tears, many live as enemies of the cross of Christ. Their destiny is destruction, their god is their stomach, and their glory is in their shame. Their mind is on earthly things. But our citizenship is in heaven. And we eagerly await a Savior from there, the Lord Jesus Christ, who, by the power that enables him to bring everything under his control, will transform our lowly bodies so that they will be like his glorious body.

"Therefore, my brothers, you whom I love and long for, my joy and crown, that is how you should stand firm in the Lord, dear friends!" (Philippians 3:17–4:1, NIV).

We need to teach ourselves to see things as they *could* be, not just as they are.

Rhythm: Maintaining Mountaintop Motivation

Is your level of motivation as high as the mountaintops...or lower than a snake's belly? As a leader, it's *your* responsibility to keep your motivation high. It's *your* responsibility to find your internal rhythm.

Leaders who lead from the inside out can feel when they're out of sync and when their motivation to keep leading is faltering. They act quickly to bring themselves back into tempo.

By *rhythm* I mean your ability to weave between the ruts and reminders like a race-car driver. It's a matter of acquiring balance. Focusing too much on the ruts leaves you unable to make any forward motion—you'll feel stuck. Focusing too much on the reminders gets you mired down in the past. You're looking for the balance that provides motivation by remembering and celebrating what God has done in your ministry but also focusing on what God's going to do.

I was watching a playoff football game some years ago in which the New York Giants experienced a meltdown and ended up going down in history as the team that gave their opponent the fifth-best comeback in NFL post-season history. The San Francisco 49ers came back from a *twenty-four-point* deficit.

Near the end of the game, when tempers were boiling, a play ended in some pushing and shoving. In fact, one of the players completely lost control of himself. After everything was sorted out, the referee explained the penalties. The ref's words that day bothered me so much that I went right to my computer to write them down.

Though the referee ejected the offending player from the game, he never used the word *ejected*. The referee simply announced, "By the nature of his actions, he has disqualified himself."

The phrase reverberated in my heart. *"By the nature of his actions, he has disqualified himself."* If we're not careful, we can experience the same thing. How crucial is self-control! How terribly important is wise internal leadership!

Our "nature" bubbles internally until it surfaces externally in our actions. If our nature is being transformed by the indwelling Spirit day by day, no problem. Our external actions will reflect what's happening in our hearts.

DIVE IN! (Questions for Reflection and Discussion)

I. Do you ever take gimmes or mulligans in some parts of your life? What are some drawbacks to this, for you and for others?

2. Think about some of the "seamy sides" of your self. What internal character concerns could you add to your prayer list this week?

3. Which ruts are your own personal favorites? Why?

4. Talk about some of the visual reminders you use to stay fired up for ministry.

5. Which of the internal reminders is most relevant to you these days? What other reminders could you add to the list by virtue of your personal ministry experience or observation?

6. What is the typical level of your motivation? What's one practical step you could take to heighten it in the coming week?

DIVING RULES AND TOOLS

Tool: *Dive computer*

Spiritual Application:
Each dive computer has two vital gauges to keep you aware of your pressure and depth. The deeper you go, the more pressure you encounter and the more air you need to survive.

It's worth our effort to stop occasionally and check our internal dive computer. At some point we all reach crush depth, when a little self-leadership would have helped us return to the surface safely.

Notes

1. The story about Christopher Reeve can be found in an interview article by Ellen N. Woods, "Nothing Is Impossible" (copyright 1997 by the American Physical Therapy Association, Inc.) at this Web site, as of May 2003: http://www.apta.org/pt_magazine/Jun97/reeve.htm

2. Adapted from Craig Brian Larson, ed., *Illustrations for Preaching and Teaching* (Grand Rapids, MI: Baker Book House, 1993), 277.

Chapter 5

Control the Flow

Growing in influence demands that you control what's influencing you.

Dive Tool: *Regulator*

You can't breathe compressed air straight out of your tank—it would explode your lungs! You need something to control the flow and the pressure, a device that makes underwater inhalation almost as easy as...breathing.

There's a little culprit in my life that can waste a lot of my time. It's called television. Can you relate?

Let's say you watch an average of four hours of television per day. Call it twenty-eight hours per week.

Now do the math. You'll lose more than *ten years* of your life to the tube if you make it to seventy years of age. Ten years or more! That's a decade of *not* communicating with your family and friends, *not* thinking creatively, *not* contributing to your church or neighborhood, *not* enriching the life of someone else.

All because of television shows.

There was a time the advice of the day was "go with the flow." But in today's fast-paced world that's full of enticing attractions and distractions, the "flow" is coming at us at an alarming rate. Going with the flow means eventually drowning in the current.

We need to control the flow instead of being swept away in it. We need to be thoroughly proactive with our schedules, social agendas, and ministry commitments.

That's why I'd like to take a different approach to time management in this chapter. I don't think we'll grow in influence simply by figuring out how to manage each minute of our days. Rather, I think we grow in influence, and become healthier leaders, when we learn to control the flow of our entire lives—what's flowing in and what's flowing out.

In scuba diving, this is where the regulator comes in.

A regulator makes it possible to use the compressed air in your tank. It reduces the tank's high-pressurized air to match the surrounding water pressure. It gives you air "on demand" when you inhale, controlling the airflow from the tank when you need it. In a sense, it resuscitates you, sustaining life and vibrancy.

Here's what Ephesians 5:15-16 (NLT) says about regulating the "flow" of our lives: "Be careful how you live, not as fools but as those who are wise. Make the most of every opportunity for doing good in these evil days."

Notice that Paul suggests we "make the most of every opportunity." We have to take some initiative. We have to choose to take action.

With a scuba regulator, you also have to make a choice because you only get air if you inhale. You have to be disciplined and proactive—or you drown. The regulator won't automatically breathe for you.

Here's what I want you to think about in this chapter:

1. What it will take for you to choose to live without wasting precious moments because you're being swept away in the fast current of your culture and life.

2. How to embrace the key questions you must answer about your priorities if you want to grow as a leader. And, for good measure...

3. Let's see how well you relate to some of my favorite "time games."

Waste Not, Want Not

Someone recently asked me, "Craig, can you walk away from an opportunity?"

I honestly didn't know how to answer that question. My natural inclination is to see every opportunity that comes my way as a door God is opening, so I push right on through. I forget to ask, "*Should* I walk through?"

Some of the things I do—that *we* do—we shouldn't be doing at all. We're simply wasting our time with these activities, squandering valuable minutes and hours that could be spent on more worthy efforts. We aren't using our time wisely. We can't get to the true opportunities God gives us because we're too busy doing all the other stuff that clutters up our lives and ministries.

Even worse, when time-stress kicks in, we start acting irritable. We develop a contagiously bad attitude. We may even feel the physical pain of the mismanagement.

Does this sound like you? Are you perpetually overwhelmed and short of breath? If so, it's time for you to clear the time-wasters from your ministry.

Here are the first five items you can give the old heave-ho—five things I suggest aren't worth doing with your time. They may help you figure out how you'll organize your next few days, but they won't help you know what's most important to do in the first place. They don't control the flow.

Time-Waster #1: *Making endless "to-do" lists.*

Some people have so many sticky notes on their computer monitors that they can't see the screen. My philosophy is if you want to jot something down, go ahead. But when your to-do list becomes your "value list," the end is near; throw away the sticky notes and burn the list.

Most of the things on our to-do lists have short-term gains and rewards. Focus instead on your *long*-range goals, and finish *big*-impact tasks first.

I don't know who said it first, but it's well worth remembering: *The urgent is never important; the important is never urgent.*

We tend to organize our lives around the urgent and unfinished. When we have a to-do list, we start from the top down, eager to scratch off the items as fast as possible.

Instead, we need to "value engineer" the items on our lists. What items will give us the best return on our investment of time and energy? Which items are really unimportant but tempting to tackle first because getting them out of the way gives us a sense of satisfaction?

If you're a list-maker, recognize that not every item you've listed is equal in terms of importance. Item number one may not have the same impact as does item number seven, but it's doubtful you wrote your list with the items sorted by significance or impact. That's a separate step most list-makers don't accomplish before jumping in and tackling tasks.

Is your life organized around the urgent and unfinished? or around impact and significant opportunities? Don't mistake crossing items off a list with accomplishing what's most important to accomplish; they usually aren't the same.

How much more would you accomplish if you organized your list by impact and opportunity? or tossed your list and just did the high-impact stuff?

Time-Waster #2: *Investing in timesaving devices.*

Ironic, isn't it? We have PalmPilots to organize our schedules, but our schedules are out of control. We have cell phones to manage our contacts, and our lives are out of control. We have all the gadgets, but are they helping us or hurting us?

Technology doesn't necessarily help us with time management. It might, but that's up to you. A word of caution: Before you run out and buy a PalmPilot or planning calendar, first determine what God wants you to accomplish during your entire ministry. Discover what he wants to create within your character. No PalmPilot or personal planner will tell you the answers to those questions.

It's odd that, in the old days, no one had a watch but everyone had time. Today everyone has a watch but no one has time. It's like Lily Tomlin has written: "The trouble with the rat race is that even if you win, you're still a rat."

It accomplishes nothing if you get to be very effective at doing the wrong things. That's not influence; it's silliness.

Time-Waster #3:
Listening when somebody begins with "You really need to..."

You've heard of the Four Spiritual Laws? The first law says, "God loves you and offers a wonderful plan for your life." In ministry, if we're not careful, we'll fall prey to that first law's less friendly twin: "God loves you, and everybody *else* has a wonderful plan for your life."

In every church there seems to be a few people who truly believe they're God's gift to you when it comes to planning your ministry. In fact, most of them believe they're God's gift to *everyone*. They're not.

Rather, they're reckless, and most of the time they don't have their own lives together. Not that it stops them from having powerful opinions about how you should organize your life and priorities.

When you encounter people like this, honor them in your conversation, smile kindly, but dismiss their advice—graciously. And by all means, don't let them waste your time.

There are people who have insight into how God might be directing your ministry. You'll recognize those people by their honest concern about the well-being of you and your ministry. They won't be nearly as interested in making their point as in serving God by sharing what they know and believe.

Time Waster #4:
Letting guilt or perfectionism motivate you to action.

Ever end up doing things that cost you valuable time even though the tasks give you little return on your investment?

Determine if you routinely do things because somebody else expects you'll do those things. I'm not talking about your boss here; if your boss wants something done, get it done.

Certain personality types just won't let themselves rest until everything is cleaned, put away, ironed, sanded, pressed, peeled, pickled, fermented, or vacuumed. Is that you? If so, sometimes you need to say, "Forget it, I'm going to bed early." Or "I'm going out to dinner."

Letting guilt or perfectionism motivate your work will cause undo stress in the long run.

Time-Waster #5:
Assuming—demanding—that you'll get it all done.

I don't want to talk to you about getting more done; I want to talk to you about doing less. You can't get it all done.

When we interview people for a job in children's ministry here at Saddleback, we always let them know that if they require a sense of closure with their work, they are probably in the wrong ministry. There's always something else that could be done or started. We must make a choice to *not* get it all done.

One reason we children's ministry folks think we aren't getting things done is the interruptions we have to endure. But C.S. Lewis helped me view the so-called interruptions that tumble into my day from a different perspective:

"Stop regarding all the unpleasant things as interruptions of [your] 'own,' or 'real' life," he wrote. "The truth is of course that what one calls the interruptions are precisely one's real life—the life God is sending one day by day."[1]

If you want to grow in your influence, you must control how you use your time. But don't settle for just filling each hour with more tasks or doing tasks more efficiently. That will help you get more done, but it won't increase your influence by itself.

Your influence grows when you do the right things—the high-impact, important things—and make room for interruptions that are really opportunities. If every minute of your day is already booked solid, how will you find time to be available for new assignments God has for you?

Confront These Questions—and Control the Flow

Controlling the flow is actually less about time management techniques and more about growing into a life orientation that values God's priorities. This means keeping certain questions in the front of our minds. Here are some questions I use. You'll develop more of your own, but I hope these will get you started.

· *Why overwork when you can simply overflow?*
We want to overflow, not overwork.

In order to have an overflow, you have to have an abundance. Let me ask you this: At the end of the day, do you have anything else left to give? If your answer is no, you're overworked. If your answer is yes, then you have overflow. Great!

· *Why follow everybody else's "calling" for you?*
When values are clear, decisions are easy.

Here's what I mean: Several years ago, at the first church in which I served, the Boy Scouts wanted to integrate their program into the church's overall ministry. I can remember the scoutmaster approaching me in the hallway one Sunday morning. Our conversation went something like this...

"Craig, I'd like to make an appointment with you."

"Sure, Phil. Can you give me a quick idea what's on your mind?"

"Well, I want to talk with you about our Boy Scouts program. I'm hoping we can work together more closely and expand the scouting program here at the church."

I thought about this for a moment and then told him a meeting wouldn't be necessary. He was pleased that I would sign on so readily, but I quickly explained to him that we didn't need to meet because the Boy Scouts wouldn't be integrating with the children's ministry at the church. His countenance fell—immediately.

"Believe me," I said. "I find nothing wrong with the Boy Scouts. I was in the scouts for a few years myself, and I loved it. I have nothing against you, your fellow leaders, your troop, or your mission."

Phil looked thoroughly confused as he scuffed a shoe back and forth over the hallway carpet. "So what's the problem then, Craig?" he asked.

"It's just that I clearly know where I want to take the children's ministry here. This is after countless hours of planning, praying, visioning, and preparing others to come alongside us. And the Boy Scouts have never factored into the equation."

Phil saw my point; he began looking at other alternatives. The time it would have taken to have a meeting and then tell him "no" wouldn't have been a great use of my time or his. And because I knew what I valued in ministry, I was able to stop the meeting before it started.

When values are clear, decisions are easy. *But don't expect people to fully understand this type of behavior.* Most live their lives at the discretion of others or according to whatever makes them feel good at the moment.

You, on the other hand, must learn to control the flow.

Don't build your life on the expectations of others. Stay focused on your calling, and bring your energy to bear on the things you are called to do, not the things that you aren't called to do. It takes preparation and determination to arrive at your destination, but the payoff is great. Consider this passage from Proverbs:

"Whoever works his land will have plenty to eat. Whoever chases unrealistic dreams will have plenty of nothing. A trustworthy person has many blessings, but anyone in a hurry to get rich will not escape punishment. Showing partiality is not good, because some people will turn on you even for a piece of bread. A stingy person is in a hurry to get rich, not realizing that poverty is about to overtake him" (Proverbs 28:19-22, GWT).

· *Why aren't you value-engineering your priorities?*

Suppose you won a contest at your local bank. Your prize: Each day at 6 a.m., $86,400 was deposited into your checking account. This happened each day for the rest of your life. The only catch: At the end of the twenty-four-hour period, anything you hadn't spent was debited from your account.

You'd want to choose wisely how to invest those dollars, for your good and the good of the world.

Now suppose each day you're given 86,400 seconds to invest. (Note: You are!) You have to choose how and where to invest those seconds every day because at the end of the day, whatever you've not invested wisely will be gone forever—without increasing your ministry's influence.

No doubt you'd take spending that $86,400 dollars each day seriously. We need to be equally serious in viewing our time as an investment because each day we get 86,400 seconds to use...or waste.

The point: Take charge of your schedule, or it will take charge of you. You must control the flow. You'll always have more things to do than you have time to do them, so be clear about what God wants you to accomplish. That's why you need to become a master at value-engineering your priorities.

In today's fast-moving, flexible society, we need to constantly re-evaluate our priorities. What takes precedence? What takes priority? When God causes an opportunity to appear that isn't in our plans, what do we do?

Here's what *not* to do: Keep working your plan, and keep God in a box.

Instead, add a new goal. Embrace a new program. Hug a new kid. Re-evaluate, re-prioritize, and value-engineer the rest of your time to be effective for Christ.

We need to pursue the right things in order to be successful. We need to continually review God's will and purpose for our lives so we can determine what activities are most worth doing.

The goal isn't to cross everything off your to-do list. The goal is to be certain of what God has called you to do and then, in light of that, evaluate your tasks and do what's necessary to fulfill your calling.

· *Why are you hurrying so fast?*

I heard a story about a sign nailed to a fence post on an Arkansas farm. It said:

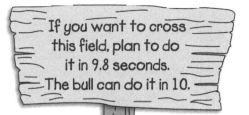

Now *that's* helpful information. If you're going to cross that field, you know exactly how fast you need to move.

It seems we're perpetually in a hurry. We rely on "speed-pass" at gas stations, shampoo and conditioner in one, cell phones, smart phones, faster cars, and pizza delivered in thirty minutes. And did I mention fast food? Not *good* food, not *cheap* food, but *fast* food. We've invented the drive-through so we can all eat in the car as God intended. We are constantly telling our kids to hurry up. We are constantly being told to hurry up.

All so we can do more, have more, go more, accomplish more. Consider this passage...

"I said, 'I have worked hard for nothing; I have used all my power, but I did nothing useful' " (Isaiah 49:4a).

Is that you? Getting a lot done, but you're not sure it's worth anything? That's a surefire way to burn out.

If you're always hurrying, I ask you to please consider these wise words from Henri J.M. Nouwen. He understood what it takes to control the flow and said it in a better way than I could as he identified what focus Christian leaders need.

"It is the discipline of dwelling in the presence of the One who keeps asking us, "Do you love me?"...Contemplative prayer deepens in us the knowledge that we...already belong to God, even though everything and everyone around us keeps suggesting the opposite."[2]

If you want to be healthy as a leader, if you want to grow in your influence, you'll need times of silence and solitude. We'll explore that further in Chapter 10. But for now, enough said?

· *Why not say NO—a lot more than you do?*

This sounds easier than it really is. From experience I've found that "yes" leads to stress and "no" leads to slow. We all could use a little slowing down in our lives. The reason this is so tough is that we are typically saying "no" to some*one*, not some*thing.*

And things don't get disappointed, but people do. A great reminder here is that Jesus modeled this approach to slowing down and focusing for us. Mark 5:37 (NLT) says, "Then Jesus stopped the crowd and wouldn't let anyone go with him except Peter and James and John."

Did you notice that? Jesus wouldn't let anyone go with him except Peter, James, and John. We often roll right over that verse, but there's something important here for us to see: *Jesus stopped the crowd.*

The text does not say how many were in the crowd, but it's clear that Jesus chose three followers from the crowd. He said "yes" to those three—Peter, James, and John. He said "no" to the rest.

Jesus said "no" to a multitude. Does that help you say "no" to just a few of the demanding folks you'll meet today?

Stop Playing Games With Your Time!

C.S. Lewis' book *The Screwtape Letters* consists of thirty-one letters from the devil Screwtape to his nephew, the devil Wormwood. In one particular letter, Screwtape told Wormwood how to render the believer useless in life and ministry. He advised his rookie nephew to stop trying to get his subject to make poor choices or do something wrong. Instead, Screwtape told Wormwood, if he wanted to render a believer useless in life and ministry, *simply keep that believer busy.*

One way we stay busy is through playing games with our time. What do I mean? Consider my descriptions below...

Trivial Pursuit

I remember when the game Trivial Pursuit first came out. It was the most popular game of its time, and we would play it for hours. The ironic thing is that most of us play this game every day with our schedules. We relentlessly pursue things that have little or no impact on our lives or the lives of others.

We forget that the goal isn't doing what's urgent. The goal is to do what's important.

The Game of Life

The goal in the Game of Life is to retire as a millionaire. That's the goal of the game, but not the goal in "real" life. The Bible is clear that investment in people is the wisest investment choice of all.

Monopoly

If you love the idea of becoming rich and influential as fast as possible, you're going to love playing Monopoly. The goal is to acquire wealth and power so you can build a financial kingdom and become the chairman of the board—ASAP.

But building God's kingdom isn't a game, and having great influence doesn't necessarily mean you'll take over the entire board. Be responsible for the *depth* of your life and ministry, and let God be responsible for the *breadth* of your life and ministry. Focus on long-term reward rather than short-term immediate gain.

Perfection

A snap to learn, Perfection is tough to play. You have to put all twenty-five different shapes into the corresponding holes of a spring-loaded tray before a sixty-second timer runs out. When the clock clangs, the tray scatters pieces all over!

We spend more time in our lives trying to make sure the right pieces go back in the right places than enjoying our interactions with other players. Our perfectionism often leads to painful isolation.

It's counterintuitive, but it makes sense: Don't pay unnecessary attention to detail if you don't need to. Rather than demanding perfection, strive for excellence, and bring others along with you.

Sorry!

I played this game often as a child. Someone would slide into my player and knock me off the board, sending me back to my home base. Then I'd hear the sarcastic, "Sorry!" ringing through the room.

I knew they weren't "sorry." They had knocked me off—intentionally!

I know it's just a game, but this is also a time-waster. Occasionally when we're offended, we hold grudges. When we hold grudges, we spend an inordinate amount of time focused on the offending party. Isn't it time to move on?

Battleship

Here's where we spend our time trying to sink our enemies. Listen, *let it go*. Focus on the positive things in life. To spend significant amounts of time arguing or doing battle over a meaningless issue isn't a good use of time. So what if the children's ministry got stiffed on a budget increase again this year? That's not a cause to attack other church workers as you attempt to wrestle resources away from them.

When you finish playing a game, it all goes back in the box. And when your life is over, *you're* going back in the box!

Don't play games with God's calling on your life. Find out what he wants you to do and do it. Don't waste your time, it's your most precious resource.

Time management is all about *what you are called to do*. It's your *calling* that helps you set meaningful goals and keeps you from wasting your time on unimportant things. Scripture reminds us:

"My brothers and sisters, try hard to be certain that you really are called and chosen by God. If you do all these things, you will never fall" (2 Peter 1:10).

Remember the Time Limit

Today God has given you 86,400 seconds to live out your life and calling. That's 168 hours to invest this week.

The question is how are you investing it? The Bible says, "Teach us to make the most of our time, so that we may grow in wisdom" (Psalm 90:12, NLT). We need to make the most of our time because we have a limited supply of it.

Yet you may have little control over the flow of things that get poured into your life, that cascade downstream and wash over you. There's your ministry, your family, your own devotional life...and reading, an occasional load of laundry, and a dental appointment you've rescheduled twice, and you find you're looking for more hours in your day.

Joshua looked for more time as well. He asked the Lord for additional time in his day, and the Lord gave it to him. As you read the following Scripture passage, pay careful attention to the closing verse, especially the part where it says, "Never before, or after..."

"The day the Lord handed the Amorites over to the people of Israel, Joshua spoke to the Lord while Israel was watching, 'Sun, stand still over Gibeon, and moon, stand still over the valley of Aijalon!' The sun stood still, and the moon stopped until a nation got revenge on its enemies. Isn't this recorded in the Book of Jashar? The sun stopped in the middle of the sky, and for nearly a day the sun was in no hurry to set. Never before or after this day was there anything like it. The Lord did what a man told him to do, because the Lord fought for Israel" (Joshua 10:12-14, GWT).

Never before *or after* has God given us extra hours...which means no matter how hard you pray for added hours in your day, it won't happen. No, you have available just what gets issued to you each and every day: 86,400 seconds.

How will you use them?

Dive In! (Questions for Reflection and Discussion)

1. How much TV do you watch each week, on average? Are you pleased with this amount?

2. Analyze your own biggest time-waster. How does it keep trapping you? What steps can you take to invest your time more wisely?

3. When was the last time you let guilt or perfectionism motivate your actions? How did things turn out?

4. Think about my conversation with the Boy Scout leader. What is your reaction? What might you do differently?

5. What is your definition of *value-engineering*? Where do you need this the most in your ministry these days?

6. What is your most obvious time-wasting "board game"? What can you do to counter the attraction of this game for you?

DIVING RULES AND TOOLS

Tool: *Regulator*

Spiritual Application:

In ministry, demands come at us from all directions. It seems that people often have their own agendas for how we should swim through our day.

Some people would like to control the way we do ministry. Though most are good-hearted people, if we let them dominate, we won't be able to breathe. The pressure will build until it's unbearable.

The "regulator" in this situation is our firm decision to control the flow of time, energy, and resources in our lives. This means breathing in a balanced mixture of ministry work, family time, worship, play, and rest.

Notes

1. C.S. Lewis, in a letter to Arthur Greeves, as quoted in Gary Wilde, *Fulfillment: Living at Peace* (Wheaton, IL: Victor Books, 1996), 49.

2. Henri J.M. Nouwen, *In the Name of Jesus* (New York: Crossroad, 1989), 28-29.

Chapter 6

Effects of Stress: Such a Mess!

It's tough to influence others when we're stressed out, defeated, and discouraged.

Dive Tool: *Fins*

Fins cover a wider surface area than our feet, so they can move us through the water with less effort. The principle is simple: Work smarter, not harder.

I was only five years old when Mom and I rode along near our home. Suddenly, she jumped out of the car and ran across the street to flag down a passing vehicle.

What's wrong?

I can remember yelling for Mom to come back, but she had a single focus. She got the car pulled over, grabbed a lunch sack the driver handed to her, and began breathing into it heavily.

What's happening to Mom? I wondered.

Today we might call it an anxiety attack, or possibly a panic attack. Either way, the effects of stress took their toll on my mom and made a lasting impression on my young mind that day.

The doctors call it hyperventilation, which is an abnormally fast or deep breathing pattern. During a panic attack, the body exhales too much carbon dioxide, which causes the blood vessels in the body to narrow, allowing less blood to circulate. If blood flow to the brain is restricted, then the anxious victim may feel dizzy or faint.

Bottom line: Whether hitting us in the form of panic, ulcers, backache, or nervous tics, the effects of stress are a mess. And anyone who says stress is "all in your head" hasn't been checking anyone's blood pressure lately!

Stress has very real physical consequences in our lives. There's a reason it's suspected of contributing to a huge percentage of medical visits. How big a percentage? Nobody knows for sure, but when you consider what impact stress has on your *own* body, you begin to get an idea. Ongoing, relentless stress can even kill you. Consider these physical responses to stress:

· Stress can affect your concentration, which leads to poor decision-making and possible danger.

· Stress can cause sleep disorders and the problems that arise from being tired and distracted.

· Stress can cause anxiety and irritability, which certainly won't help your relationships.

· Stress can contribute to digestive problems.

· Stress can lead to excessive weight gain or weight loss.

· Stress can be a key factor in producing headaches, high blood pressure, heart disease, and perhaps even cancer.

· Stress can weaken the immune system, making you more susceptible to colds and other diseases.

True, stress may be in your head. But it sets up branch offices all over your body.

Why All the Stress?

We all respond uniquely to life's "negative" events and relationships. But as different as we all are, there are some common stressors that seem to impact all of us.

Financial difficulties, for instance, send chills up the spine of pretty much everyone. Then there are such things as unmet or unrealistic expectations (you expected the raise but didn't get it); painful relationships (you experience sudden or ongoing betrayal, lack of loyalty, or rejection); negative people (you keep having to bear the brunt of pessimism and disapproval); or an approval orientation (you have a need to please others, regardless of your own needs).

What is it for you? What are the particular stress buttons that can set you off into spirals of swirling anxiety?

A Quick Test:

Stress is the result of carrying too great a weight, day after day. Is stress becoming strain in your life?

Do you have trouble making simple decisions?
Do you have thoughts of escaping to some other place?
Do you have a hard time finishing a thought?
Do you have a hard time creating a thought?
Do you live with the fear of having a heart attack?
Do you experience sudden mood swings?
Do you feel as if you're always out of energy?
Do you have continual feelings of inadequacy?

We all know people who have a hard time with stress—maybe a harder time than most of us. Let me tell you about six people I've known in athletics (I played college baseball) who practically made stress a varsity sport. Yes, they brought it on themselves, but perhaps we can still learn from their experiences and approaches to life.

These men basically describe six personality types that will have a difficult time with stress. Do you see your own personality in any of them?

Battling Bob: "Just don't put me down; I mean it!"

He was a good ballplayer with lots of natural talent. But his performance always seemed to suffer after some sportswriter criticized his play. Bob simply couldn't handle criticism. When he read a story that pointed out a ball he'd dropped or a play he'd handled badly, he wanted to do battle with the writer. His temper would burst into flames at the least hint of criticism.

Sensitive Sam: "What if I blow it again? Oh, no! I did!"

Sam wasn't a bad player, but he was so aware of his weaknesses on the field that he spent most of his time trying to avoid making mistakes. That's no way to play good baseball. Focusing too much on your weaknesses can cause huge stress.

Pedestal Pete:
"Look at me, everybody! (I really need you to look, guys!)"

Pete was the all-conference ballplayer. He was good—very good—and he let everyone inside a ten-mile radius know it. No matter what the topic of discussion, Pete turned it to baseball so he could recount his latest triumphs. Pete was proud, but not of the team or the sport or even the chance to do well. He was proud of himself, period. Pete built a pedestal, climbed up on it, and crowed to the world. And once up there, Pete had to *stay* there—a difficult assignment.

Disappointed Don:
"Can I go in now, Coach? Can I? Can I? What about now?"

Every team has the last guy picked for the squad, and everyone knows who that guy is. For us, it was Don. Yes, he'd made the team, which was quite an accomplishment. But he spent most games sitting on the bench, waiting to get called into a game. The problem: Don didn't accept his role as a utility player. He could have focused on contributing as a helper and encourager to the other players. Instead, his ambition far outweighed his abilities. He lived season after season of constant disappointment.

Jealous Jake: "Some guys just get all the breaks!"

To say that Jake was jealous of others' accomplishments would be like saying water is damp. The guy was constantly seething. If a pitcher had thrown that fast ball to *him*, instead of to the *other* guy, he'd have hit the game-winning shot. Jealousy ate away at Jake. He always wanted to be best, and sometimes that led to chipping away at the reputations of other players.

Greedy Gary: "Outta my way! Back off! I got it already!"

A well-rounded ballplayer and a nice enough guy, but Gary was grasping. By that I mean he had a "me-first" attitude that showed itself in everything from demanding a specific seat on the team bus to diving in front of another player to snag an outfield catch. Gary was the only college player I knew who had an agent: *himself*. He was always grasping for another or better opportunity, a larger piece of the pie.

In many ways each of these players influenced his college baseball team. But the influence wasn't positive. The stress of having to constantly perform well caused these players to seek unhealthy ways to make their influence known...and the team was poorer for it.

We're influencing our worlds, too, and stress can impact how we use our influence. For people in ministry, stress comes with the territory. But we get to choose *how* to respond to stress.

Consider this advice from the book of Jude:

"But you, dear friends, must continue to build your lives on the foundation of your holy faith" (Jude 1:20a, NLT).

If we're honest, we'll admit that we don't often take time to intentionally build our own lives. We're busy helping kids, neighbors, small groups, or our church family. So we put our needs, for the most part, at the far end of a very long to-do list. We don't tend to our health physically or spiritually. We don't get around to praying. Or exercising. Or being silent before God. And since we can only lead others as far as we've gone ourselves, we limit the impact and influence of our ministries and leadership.

An Action Plan: Strip the Strain From Stress!

The St. John River is 450 miles long and empties into the Bay of Fundy in St. John, New Brunswick, Canada. What's amazing about this river is that each day the river flows downstream and into the bay. The bay, at low tide, is fourteen feet lower than the natural level of the river.

But when tides in the bay begin to rise, they interrupt the flow of the river until it has completely stopped flowing. Perfectly calm. Experts call this *slack tide*. It's the only time during the day that boats can safely be on the falls. Just *after* slack tide, the bay continues to rise, forcing the river to flow in reverse!

The force is so strong that rapids develop in the opposite direction. The high tide actually rises fourteen feet higher than the river, causing these reversing rapids.[1]

There's an analogy here that we can apply to our busyness: *We can do things that raise the spiritual bay in our lives.* When we practice these things, "reversing rapids" occur. Our spiritual "bay" rises higher than our stress and strain. Then, slowly and steadily, the raging rapids reverse.

Here's where our diving fins come into the picture.

Fins help us work smarter, not harder, because they cover a wider surface area than our feet, creating a greater push through the water with much less effort. The principle is to *work smarter, not harder*. When we reduce stress, we can do more with less.

What are things you need to do to "raise the bay" in your life and to reverse the overwhelming flow that sometimes threatens to drown you?

I want to give you a prescription (thus all the P's) to try. These work for me, and I've seen their power in my life. So consider the following as a six-step action plan if you're living a stressful, hurried life that could use a bit more control, margin, balance, and health.

I. Prefer a Proper Perspective ("I'm only human.")

You don't have to do it all. God was doing fine before you came along. He's doing fine with you. And he'll be doing fine when you're gone. When it comes to keeping the universe spinning, God doesn't actually require your assistance, nor has he delegated the task to you.

We often try to do it all. We're ministry-minded, so we're wired that way. We tackle every opportunity that comes along, and as believers we put a scriptural spin on it, saying, "I can do all things through Christ who gives me strength."

Fine...but you often start the day saying, "I can do it all," and finish the day saying, "What happened? I didn't get it all done." Little interruptions that come into your day—interruptions that weren't planned—kept you from completing every task you thought important to finish.

Did Jesus fail you? Did he *not* give you the strength to do all things?

Don't worry—Jesus didn't fail. The problem isn't with Jesus. It's with us.

We tend to forget what Jesus wants us to do—be faithful and obedient. That part we understand. But we need to also add this: Be *available*. He wants us to know our calling and be available to be interrupted at any time to take care of an opportunity he puts before us. Sometimes the most faithful, obedient thing we can do is throw our to-do list out the window.

Both Jesus and his followers—like us—have roles and responsibilities. Some things are mine to do. Some things are Jesus' to do. The bottom line is we're not God. When we try to act like we are by assuming too much control, stress sets in big time. It's always good to keep the proper perspective here.

So ask yourself this question when you're doing ministry and living your life: Is this *my* issue, or is this *Jesus'* issue?

When a child accepts Jesus as Savior, is that my issue or Jesus' issue?

When a decision moves us ahead but doesn't please everyone inside fifty miles of the church, is that my issue or Jesus' issue?

When a program is successful far beyond our most hopeful plans, is that my issue or Jesus' issue?

Let me give you an example of how this works. We'll consider the time Jesus raised Lazarus from the dead. Here's what happened...

"But Mary went to the place where Jesus was. When she saw him, she fell at his feet and said, 'Lord, if you had been here, my brother would not have died.'

"When Jesus saw Mary crying and the Jews who came with her also crying, he was upset and was deeply troubled. He asked, 'Where did you bury him?'

" 'Come and see, Lord,' they said.

"Jesus cried.

"So the Jews said, 'See how much he loved him.'

"But some of them said, 'If Jesus opened the eyes of the blind man, why couldn't he keep Lazarus from dying?'

"Again feeling very upset, Jesus came to the tomb. It was a cave with a large stone covering the entrance. Jesus said, 'Move the stone away.'

"Martha, the sister of the dead man, said, 'But, Lord, it has been four days since he died. There will be a bad smell.'

"Then Jesus said to her, 'Didn't I tell you that if you believed you would see the glory of God?'

"So they moved the stone away from the entrance. Then Jesus looked up and said, 'Father, I thank you that you heard me. I know that you always hear me, but I said these things because of the people here around me. I want them to believe that you sent me.' After Jesus said this, he cried out in a loud voice, 'Lazarus, come out!' The dead man came out, his hands and feet wrapped with pieces of cloth, and a cloth around his face.

"Jesus said to them, 'Take the cloth off of him and let him go' " (John 11:32-44).

Let's look at this passage from the "my issue/Jesus' issue" perspective. We might draw conclusions like these:

Jesus' Issue: Jesus asked a question: "Where did you bury him?"
Fact: Lazarus had died, and Jesus asked where they had buried him.
My Issue: Respond to Jesus with an answer: "Come and see him."

Jesus' Issue: Jesus gave a command to be followed: "Move the stone away."
Fact: Jesus watched while the people moved the stone back from the tomb.
My Issue: Obey Jesus and move the stone.

Jesus' Issue: Jesus issued a command: "Lazarus, come out!"
Fact: Jesus brought Lazarus back to life.
My Issue: Sit back and watch the miracle unfold. There's nothing I have to do to contribute to the cause—I'm just along for the ride.

Jesus' Issue: Jesus issued a command: "Take the cloth off of him and let him go."
Fact: Lazarus was alive but bound; he was stumbling around.
My Issue: Obey Jesus and unbind Lazarus. And, I think, learn from what I've seen and ask myself this: What do I need to "unbind" in my own life in order to do more than just stumble around?

We aren't dead, but we *are* bound by things that cause stress and strain in our lives. We need a proper perspective about stress.

Can we agree that suddenly being raised from the dead was stressful for Lazarus? It was an unexpected change, to say the least. Yet it was undoubtedly a welcome change.

Part of our perspective about stress should include the fact that some stress is actually good for us. If you lift weights, you know that when your muscles are stressed during a workout, then given proper rest, you become stronger. It's when you overwork your muscles without proper rest—or try to over-lift—that you end up straining muscles.

We're going to have problems and trials in our lives. God allows these things that we might develop endurance and a stronger faith in his goodness and power. James, chapter 1, teaches us that. It's part of the program.

However, when we allow stress to become strain and strain to become pain, our minds and bodies won't function as they should. We won't be learning faith; we'll be ineffective and broken.

2. Push the Pause Button ("How about a brief timeout?")

"It's useless to rise early and go to bed late, and work your worried fingers to the bone. Don't you know he enjoys giving rest to those he loves?" (Psalm 127:2, *The Message*).

Notice that I suggest you "pause," not that you "stop." For you hard-driving, full-ahead, type-A personalities, there may not be much difference. Either option is painful for you.

I've found that for me to pause requires a certain level of discipline, and the best way for me to pause is to withdraw and spend some time in silence and solitude.

I want to be sure you know what I'm *not* saying here. I'm *not* saying that you should hold things in and be alone so you can lick your wounds. I *am* saying that it often helps you find balance and health as a leader if you'll spend a certain amount of time in silence and a certain amount of time in solitude. Solitude is being alone, all by yourself. Not in the presence of another. Silence is simply being quiet—no talking, no sound, nothing. Silent.

My sons are quite the communicators. Since they're only in kindergarten, they have an unending capacity to talk and make sounds, noises, and anything else that has an audible tone to it. My wife, Mary, and I occasionally have had to put both of our sons in what we call a "talking timeout." We had to quickly revise it to an "any-sound-at-all-is-prohibited timeout." Sure, they stopped talking, but all the other grunts, burps, car sounds, train sounds, airplane sounds, and you-name-it sounds continued to roll.

I suggest that we all need not only a talking timeout but also an any-kind-of-noise timeout. Silence is the absence of sound; it's stillness, quietness. Jesus himself often carved out times of silent retreat because he knew the importance of taking a pause in his ministry life to catch his breath, recalibrate, and then move on.

For example, after Jesus fed the five thousand—after an intense burst of ministry energy—he chose to be alone.

"About five thousand men had eaten from those five loaves, in addition to all the women and children!

"Immediately after this, Jesus made his disciples get back into the boat and cross to the other side of the lake while he sent the people home. Afterward he went up into the hills by himself to pray. Night fell while he was there alone" (Matthew 14:21-23, NLT).

Jesus also sought solitude after hearing about John's death.

"When Jesus heard about John, he left in a boat and went to a place where he could be alone. The crowds heard about this and followed him on foot from the cities" (Matthew 14:13, GWT).

Did you catch that last line? The crowds *followed* him.

Here is the simple fact: Whenever you try to seek some solitude in life, someone will try to find you. And Jesus didn't even have a cell phone. We're more connected than Jesus was, but being totally wired isn't all that it's cracked up to be. You may need to *turn it off* occasionally so the crowds can't follow you.

Don't fall for the idea that "when I work, I am being productive; and when I sit and ponder alone, I am lazy." It's simply not true. Jesus not only followed intense bursts of ministry with solitude but also followed discouraging times with solitude.

For those of us who like to continue to move at warp speed with our hair on fire, great. Most of the time, our motives are pure. We do it to have a big "ER" ministry or a fast "ER" program or a better "ER" outreach program or a nice "ER" facility or to be strong "ER" leaders. And those things are all good. In fact, they can be great!

But if you keep pursuing tasks with unabated energy, always dialing it up a notch to go faster, better, bigger, stronger, you'll end up in the clean "ER" room at the hospital. Guaranteed.

3. Participate in a Weekly Worship Service ("Get me to the church on time!")

Tony lived in Rome as a young man, but he then moved to New York. In time he married, and when his son was ten, he took the boy to Rome to show the lad Daddy's old neighborhood.

As they walked down the street, Tony pointed out a shoe repair shop. "When we were young, we didn't buy new shoes every year," he said. "We economized. We had old Pino there fix our shoes. In fact, I went there so often that he might remember me."

The man and his son walked into the dark, tiny shop where shoes filled cubicles from the floor to the ceiling.

It had been twenty years, but Pino flashed a smile at the man. "Ah, little Tony!" he cried. The two men embraced, Tony introduced his boy, and Tony shook his head in amazement.

"I didn't really think you'd remember me," Tony said.

"I never forget a customer," Pino bragged, puffing out his chest.

"Customer? But I haven't walked in here since I moved away twenty years ago."

"And before you did, you left me a pair of brown leather shoes to mend," Pino said.

Tony slapped his forehead. "That's right! Unbelievable! I forgot to pick them up. Goodness," Tony said, reaching for his wallet. "How much do I owe you?"

"I'm not sure," Pino said. "I haven't gotten to them yet. Come back next Friday."

The effects of stress are serious enough that we need to act now, not wait twenty years—or even twenty minutes.

We need to rest, relax, and refresh. We need to follow intense bursts of ministry energy with times of rest. That is what the Day of Rest, Sunday, is all about.

"You should not stay away from the church meetings, as some are doing, but you should meet together and encourage each other" (Hebrews 10:25a).

I do remember what most of the people reading this book do on Sundays: coordinate or run children's ministry programs. And I'm well aware that Sunday is showtime—the busiest day of the week.

But that's no excuse for missing church and being refreshed and encouraged by the relationships we find there—with God and with people.

For us children's ministry folks, it's a constant temptation to skip a worship service here and there because we're nearby doing something in children's ministry. That's about the best possible excuse for missing a church service: "I needed to be doing something else to serve kids here at church. It was important. It made a difference for kids." Who's going to argue with that?

I will.

We can become so busy that we cut out the very things that bring balance and focus into our lives. The Bible says, "Reverence for God adds hours to each day" (Proverbs 10:27a, *TLB*). When you see yourself and your life's calling against the backdrop of eternity, it becomes easier for you to make choices about how to spend your time. You may have to leave some things undone to get to a service. Don't cut corners here. Get to a service before the singing ends. (You *know* who you are.)

4. Praise the Lord ("Crank up the volume!")

"Sing to the Lord a new song! Sing to the Lord, all the earth!" (Psalm 96:1, GWT).

I was driving on my way to a breakfast meeting at 6:50 in the morning, and I had a CD cranked up to full volume. I was lost in my own world; I had the window down and the sunroof back. It was a beautiful California morning.

Our SUV sound-system has a pretty good resonance to anyone within fifteen feet. You can't hear me coming a mile away, but, at the top volume, you can hear me coming. And you can hear the lyrics of the music.

I'd pulled up to a light, and the song "His Love Endures Forever" was crankin'. When I looked back out the rear passenger window, the guy in the car next to me and back a little had his window open and was signing the song, verbatim. The back windows are tinted in my car, so I could see him but he couldn't see me.

The look on his face wasn't stress.

It's amazing what a well-positioned car with a CD player and the right timing can do. We were both rejoicing in the Lord. I felt the need to drive alongside him until the song was over.

I've found that when I sing to the Lord, even though I'm off key (I can't carry a tune in a bucket), my problems disappear and my stress dissipates. I can't have stress and be active in worship at the same time.

When we praise the Lord, we see how big God really is. Our stress pales in comparison.

5. Party and Have Fun ("Eat, drink, and enjoy life!")

"There is a time to cry and a time to laugh. There is a time to be sad and a time to dance" (Ecclesiastes 3:4, NCV).

I'm not going to spend a lot of time here because if I have to explain this one to you, you may need a twelve-step "How to Have Fun" program.

"And this is not all that is meaningless in our world. In this life, good people are often treated as though they were wicked, and wicked people are often treated as though they were good. This is so meaningless!

"So I recommend having fun, because there is nothing better for people to do in this world than to eat, drink, and enjoy life. That way they will experience some happiness along with all the hard work God gives them" (Ecclesiastes 8:14-15, NLT).

Is ministry fun for you? Not just joyful or purposeful—but fun? If not, I'll bet your stress meter is on overload.

Look, ministry is serious stuff, but loving God is fun. Working with volunteers is fun. Kids are a blast. And heartfelt laughing goes a long way toward building health.

6. Prize Your Private Time With God ("Where's my Bible?")

Seek daily time in God's Word.

I've found that when I spend more time in God's Word, I actually get more time back. It's ironic because when I'm extremely busy, I usually find ways to skimp on certain things in my life. Quiet time can be one of them. However, spending time in God's Word is actually an investment that pays dividends.

The psalmist says, "Your word is a lamp for my feet and a light for my path" (Psalm 119:105, NLT). I remember going camping in the mountains here in Southern California several years ago. We were playing a game with some of the youth. The rules called for somebody to go hide and then sneak back into the camp undetected.

I was sitting out in the forest that night, all by myself. At one point, when the clouds covered the moon, it was pitch black. I couldn't see my hand in front of my face, but I could hear the sound of the folks who had made it back into camp without getting caught. Yet I was stranded behind a rock and couldn't see to take another step. *If only I had a flashlight!* I thought.

I ended up fumbling around in the darkness until I made my way back to camp. Once I got back, I retrieved my flashlight and aimed it back up to where I'd been hiding. Sure enough, there was a straight path back down into camp that would have taken me five minutes to traverse. But, no, it took me an *hour* to wander my way around the mountain before making it back. Poor use of time? Yep. Would a flashlight have helped? Yep. God's Word gives us that type of guidance all along the path of life, even in our darkest moments.

Do yourself a favor: If you need more time back in your schedule, spend more time in God's Word. It will make you aware of where you should be walking in life.

I complete a five-part process when I have my quiet time. I write these headings out in my journal: Read, Reflect, Respond, Request, Remember. Could that work for you?

When I was younger, one of the guys that built into my life was an avid Scripture memory person. He always had a 3x5 card in his back pocket. Since I spent a lot of time with him, I picked up on this behavior and started memorizing. We would hold each other accountable for verses we were learning.

During those early years, God changed my heart and life because of the verses I had hidden in my heart. The following are some great verses on stress, anxiety, and the power of God.

If stress is an ongoing issue in your life and leadership, I want to suggest you memorize these verses and reflect on what they mean in your life.

"Be anxious for nothing, but in everything by prayer and supplication with thanksgiving let your requests be made known to God.

"And the peace of God, which surpasses all comprehension, will guard your hearts and your minds in Christ Jesus" (Philippians 4:6-7, NASB).

"A person's anxiety will weigh him down, but an encouraging word makes him joyful" (Proverbs 12:25, GWT).

"Act like people with good sense and not like fools. These are evil times, so make every minute count" (Ephesians 5:15-16, Contemporary English Version).

"Life is hard, but there is a time and a place for everything" (Ecclesiastes 8:6, CEV).

"Teach us to make the most of our time, so that we may grow in wisdom" (Psalm 90:12, NLT).

"Peace of mind makes the body healthy, but jealousy is like a cancer" (Proverbs 14:30, Today's English Version).

"Come to me, all who are tired from carrying heavy loads, and I will give you rest" (Matthew 11:28, GWT).

"We are often troubled, but not crushed; sometimes in doubt, but never in despair; there are many enemies, but we are never without a friend; and though badly hurt at times, we are not destroyed" (2 Corinthians 4:8-9, TEV).

Stress happens when I try to carry more than I was designed for, while neglecting my relationship with God and his Word. It happens when I forget to be available to God and am unwilling to shelve my plans to pursue his.

Learn to Rest—and Transform

Resting transforms us into what God wants us to be. The psalmist says it well: "It's useless to rise early and go to bed late, and work your worried fingers to the bone. Don't you know he enjoys giving rest to those he loves?" (Psalm 127:2, *The Message*).

A friend told me this story that captures the essence of transformation:

A family of five was visiting the United States from a Third World country, and they found themselves inside a huge shopping mall. The wife went off to explore the stores, while the father and his youngest son stood in amazement at the sight of this magnificent place. They were amazed by almost everything they saw but were especially amazed by two shiny, silver walls that could move apart and then back together again.

The boy asked, "What is that, Father?"

"Son, I have never seen anything like this in my life. I don't know what it is!"

While the boy and his father were watching the moving walls, an elderly lady with a walker approached and pressed a button. The walls opened and the lady walked between them into a small room. The walls closed, and the boy and his father watched small circles of lights with numbers above the walls light up—one, two, three.

Both father and son continued to watch the circles light up in the reverse direction—three, two, one. The walls opened up again, and a beautiful, twenty-something young lady stepped out of the room.

Without hesitation the father turned to his son and said, "Go get your mother."

Now *that's* transformation! The man watching the elevator had the wrong idea but the right process in mind.

Certainly an elevator won't transform anyone, but God's Word and the Holy Spirit can. It's what the Christian life is all about, allowing the power of the Spirit to transform our lives into all that is pleasing to Christ. If you could ask God to transform your life to one of margin and balance, would you let him do it?

We are challenged in Romans to consider this new way of thinking.

"Don't copy the behavior and customs of this world, but let God transform you into a new person by changing the way you think. Then you will know what God wants you to do, and you will know how good and pleasing and perfect his will really is" (Romans 12:2, NLT).

I remember my biology class in high school. At the beginning of the year, each study group was assigned a project. My group's project called for observing the life stages of a caterpillar; specifically, the silk worm.

We fed one a steady diet of mulberry leaves and provided the right environment for growth. As we observed its behavior over the next few weeks, it simply ate, grew, and eventually spun a cocoon.

It takes approximately three days of nonstop spinning to finish a cocoon. After the cocoon was complete and the silkworm stopped spinning, it started the process of transformation. That process takes about three weeks.

The silkworm takes a break after an intense period of "spinning" and then and *only* then does it transform—using its "down" time.

Maybe it's time we took a lesson from the silkworm. Most of us have been spinning for years. It's time to allow the cocoon of the Holy Sprit to transform our workaholic tendencies into something with wings.

Dive In! (Questions for Reflection and Discussion)

1. What are the most stressful aspects of your ministry life these days? your overall life? What are your primary coping methods?

2. Of the six ballplayers described, which comes closest to describing your style? What small step could you take to move toward improvement this week?

3. Review the six-step action plan for the hurried life. In your opinion, what are some strengths and weaknesses in this plan? How might you modify it to make it more relevant to your unique situation?

4. How would you describe your relationship with God and his Word these days?

5. How could others in your small group pray for you during the week ahead?

DIVING RULES AND TOOLS

Tool: *Fins*

Spiritual Application:
Our fins cover a wider surface area than our feet, thus creating a greater area to propel us through the water with little effort. The principle is "work smarter, not harder."
By reducing stress, you do more with less.

> "Cutting logs with a dull ax makes you work harder. A wise man will sharpen his ax. In the same way, wisdom can make any job easier" (Ecclesiastes 10:10, ICB).

Notes
1. Find information about the St. John River in the links at this Web site: http://new-brunswick.net/new-brunswick/enter.html

Part III: Vulnerability
(Social Growth)
People liked him... (Luke 2:52c)

Chapter 7

Humility, and How I Attained It

To be vulnerable to people around you and to God, you have to embrace humility...whatever the cost.

Dive Tool: *Wet suit*

The Bible reminds us that we are in the world but not of the world. We need a layer of insulation to protect us from the cold temperatures that arrogance can produce in us. The reminder for all of us is to "suit up" as we enter the waters of ministry.

My humility lesson started on my first day at Saddleback Church and then continued for the next...*year*. Yes, a training class that lasted a long, long 365 days. And it really intensified at winter camp.

We'd signed up fifty kids, which was nowhere near our potential, and we were begging adults to volunteer for the weekend. We were cutting deals like there was no tomorrow just to get people to go. We managed to pull it off and get to camp.

My problem? I was new, and few people knew my name. They didn't respect my leadership. They pushed, pulled, and poked. They made smart comments and displayed a general disrespect for who I was.

And that was the adult leaders.

The *kids* took it to a whole new level, with everything coming to a head on a bright Saturday afternoon when I wanted to buy some licorice. I strolled over to the Snack Shack with my mouth watering for red licorice. I walked up to the counter at about 3:55, knowing the Shack closed at 4.

"Sorry. We're closed," said one of the high school students who was running the place.

"Very funny. Now, I'd like two pieces of licorice, please."

"We're closed."

"You're hilarious," I said. "Two pieces, please."

The student tuned me out for about a minute, arranging boxes of Cracker Jacks and Hot Tamales on the shelf behind him. At that point, I still thought he was just joking around with the children's pastor.

"Hey, *really*. I would like two pieces of licorice, and I would like to have them now if I could."

"Nope."

Now I was close to the end of my rope, and I told him just how close I was. And that red-haired, freckle-faced kid still didn't budge. And then I said these six words, words that changed my life:

"Do you know who I AM?"

In other words: I am not a kid, I am not a volunteer, I am not even a part-time staff member; I am *the pastor.* I am in charge here. I am the one leading this entire camp.

Then I walked off.

Without my licorice.

Throughout the rest of that afternoon, things got worse for me. What churning internal turmoil! Later that night, around midnight, I was in bed in our room above the kitchen, just lying there wide awake. I was doing some serious wrestling with God, reminding him of what a terrible mistake it was for me to come to Saddleback in the first place—and that it was mostly his fault. I reminded him that people knew who I was back at my other church. I was well-liked, respected, honored, valued. Now look!

As the wrestling match continued, I reached the pinnacle of frustration around 2:00 a.m. I thought my wife had been asleep for hours as I reached the end of the rope, tied a knot, and held on. I said in a soft voice, "Whatever you're teaching me, do it quickly because I can't take this anymore."

Then, from my supposedly asleep wife, came the resounding response, *"Amen!"*

What Does a Humble Person Look Like?

I wish I could say that my humility lesson ended after that year. Instead, I've been involved in a continuous "humility workshop" ever since. Yes, the goal for me—and for you—is to become a humble person. You'd think we'd nail it one time and remember, but usually the process lasts a lifetime.

This daunting challenge started in the Garden of Eden, where a couple of human beings thought they could be like God; the essence of arrogance. From that day forward we've all asked in one form or another, "Do you know who I am?"

Here's what I've learned about asking that question: If you have to tell someone who you *are*, you *aren't.* In fact, we all "aren't." John 3:30 (NLT) says, "He must become greater and greater, and I must become less and less."

Apparently humility isn't optional for people who follow Jesus—even church leaders.

Imagine being told the most humble man in the world is coming over to visit you. You'd expect him to knock very quietly on the door, enter with his head bowed, and meekly shuffle to that chair in the far corner of the room, right?

Yet the Torah says Moses was the most humble man who ever lived. Moses, the awesome leader who stood up to Pharaoh and said, "Let my people go!" The mighty Moses who raised his staff to split the sea. The commander-in-chief who led his nation to victory in all-out war. Can you imagine Moses walking into your home? You'd be bowled over by his greatness. But still he was humble.

Our culture has mistaken *humility* for *poor,* or for *wishy-washy.* Nothing could be further from the truth.

As leaders, we need to grow in humility because without it we're useless. Without it we're far from Christlike. Without it we'll never be truly vulnerable to the people around us or to God.

I've devised an acrostic (one of my favorite teaching techniques) to help me remember some of the qualities that are found in genuinely humble people.

So I give you "H.U.M.I.L.I.T.Y." in eight easy installments:

Humble people will...
Honor others above themselves.

It all hinges on how you see yourself. Have you ever looked at a picture of yourself and thought, "Who *is* that?" A picture reveals who you really are. You may think of yourself as that physically perfect person you were a few years ago, but pictures don't lie.

You stare at the photo and find yourself thinking...

Is my hair really that long?
Am I really that short?
Is my face really that wide?
Is my head really that bald?
Is my nose really that large?
(Insert your favorite body-image issue here...)

Here's the point: Honoring others above ourselves begins with us picturing ourselves in new ways. The good news is that God has sketched some appropriate new pictures for us in Scripture.

· Picture yourself in the second chair.

"Be good friends who love deeply; practice playing second fiddle" (Romans 12:10, *The Message*).

· Picture yourself under God's hand.

"Therefore humble yourselves under the mighty hand of God, that He may exalt you at the proper time" (I Peter 5:6, NASB).

· Picture yourself with renewed health.

"Don't be impressed with your own wisdom. Instead, fear the Lord and turn your back on evil. Then you will gain renewed health and vitality" (Proverbs 3:7-8, NLT).

William Temple, archbishop of Canterbury in the 1940s, once said: "Humility does not mean thinking less of yourself than of other people, nor does it mean having a low opinion of your own gifts. It means freedom from thinking about yourself at all."[1]

I like that. And I think it's interesting how God created our bodies. Have you noticed that he made it tough to pat your own back? But it's easy to pat the backs of others.

Let's focus on encouraging, inspiring, and offering comfort. That's what honoring others is all about. And that's what humility is all about.

Humble people will...
Understand their strengths and weaknesses.

Humble people have a realistic sense of their strengths and weaknesses. Realizing that God's power shows up best in weak people, they have a healthy sense of self while keeping pride at bay. As the Apostle James wrote, "Humble yourselves before the Lord, and he will lift you up" (James 4:10, NIV).

I've accumulated quite a bit of personal experience in the struggle-to-understand-my-strengths-and-weaknesses department. A prime example is my high school speech class. I cut that class so many times that I was in serious danger of flunking it. I just *did not* want to stand in front of eighteen classmates and talk.

It was unthinkable to picture myself in the front of that class. There was no way. I wasn't going to do it. It was easier to cut the class. Of course, that meant I was planning to be the world's oldest living high school senior because speech class was required for graduation.

About three or four months into my junior year, I became a Christian. I was always a pretty good kid throughout my high school days. I don't have one of those amazing testimonies that involves escaping from prison, robbing a bank, holding up in a hotel room, deciding to end it all, attempting to jump from the third floor of the hotel only to catch my foot on the curtains, slamming into the balcony below, ricocheting through the window and landing on a Gideon Bible which just so happened to be open to John 3:16.

Nope, not me. I was a pretty good kid from day one.

But eventually I recognized that I needed a Savior, and I asked Christ to come into my life. My personality, to this day, is distinctly introverted. But I felt that once the Holy Spirit came to indwell my life that I should start...well, *speaking* about it.

I didn't want to do that. Yet I can remember going back into my speech class and doing a talk on "If you don't believe in Jesus, you will burn." I'd just become a Christian, so the theology was a bit blunt, but I was doing the best I could with what I knew.

After that performance I wasn't called on to give many more speeches in that class.

It's ironic: I know God has given me the ability to communicate verbally because it's certainly not something I was born with. Even today I get cold hands and become generally freaked out when I have to speak to a group of people. Yet, several times a year, I walk up to a microphone and speak to large groups.

And here's the true irony: Occasionally I become arrogant about God's gift to me and, within my most sinister self, I will think, *That was pretty good delivery, Craig; look what you've done.*

What a nut! Although we may understand our strengths and weaknesses, we still occasionally can get sucked into believing that it's all about us. I need to remember I Corinthians 4:7 (NLT), which says, "What makes you better than anyone else? What do you have that God hasn't given you? And if all you have is from God, why boast as though you have accomplished something on your own?"

Ouch. There's a humility-maker.

Here are three good reminders for all of us.

1. Understand that we all have strengths; all of our gifts and abilities originate in Christ.

Consider these passages:

"A spiritual gift is given to each of us as a means of helping the entire church" (I Corinthians 12:7, NLT).

"It is the one and only Holy Spirit who distributes these gifts. He alone decides which gift each person should have" (I Corinthians 12:11, NLT).

Pretty clear, isn't it? We can be excellent stewards of our strengths, but it's wrongheaded to think that they started with us. They didn't. Our strengths started with God.

2. Understand the importance of weakness; weakness in our lives keeps arrogance in check.

Paul was a talented guy, but he understood weaknesses, too—and how God could use them.

"Each time he said, 'No. But I am with you; that is all you need. My power shows up best in weak people.' Now I am glad to boast about how weak I am; I am glad to be a living demonstration of Christ's power, instead of showing off my own power and abilities" (2 Corinthians 12:9, *TLB*).

Weaknesses can keep you humble, so don't ignore them.

3. Understand that weakness keeps us depending upon God.

God allows crises into our lives to refine our character and put us in a better position to help and encourage others. In humility, we bow to this heavenly plan.

"Because of the extravagance of those revelations, and so I wouldn't get a big head, I was given the gift of a handicap to keep me in constant touch with my limitations. Satan's angel did his best to get me down; what he in fact did was push me to my knees. No danger then of walking around high and mighty!" (2 Corinthians 12:7, *The Message*).

Humble people will...
Manage their emotions.

Someone once said if you want to test a person's character, watch him when he's facing difficulty. I say if you want to test a person's character, give him success.

Sometimes we start believing our own press. When we do conferences, people tell us how good we are or how much they have been blessed or helped by what we have said or done. When we start hearing that stuff repeatedly, we can start believing it.

I remember reading the sports articles while I was a freshman playing baseball in college. I was once voted "Athlete of the Week" as a freshman. After reading my own press, I started thinking I was actually better than I really was. *What a great article,* I thought. *Hey, this Jutila's pretty good after all.* In the next five games, I batted goose eggs—went zero for eighteen! My dad later reminded me, "Don't read your own press, Craig."

Most often our emotions dictate our actions, and that's where we get ourselves into trouble. Better to act our way into feeling rather than feel our way into acting. Here are a couple of verses that will help us focus on the right response to the successes we all occasionally experience. They're all reminders that humility is the correct response to success.

"Before his downfall a man's heart is proud, but humility comes before honor" (Proverbs 18:12, NIV).

"The purity of silver and gold is tested by putting them in the fire; the purity of human hearts is tested by giving them a little fame" (Proverbs 27:21, *The Message*).

"Don't brag about yourself—let others praise you" (Proverbs 27:2, CEV).

"Don't assume that you know it all" (Proverbs 3:7a, *The Message*).

Humble people will...
Involve others.

People who have a strong leadership gift or many years of experience tend to stop relying on the counsel of others. The thinking often goes like this: *I've been right most of the time in the past, so why should I question myself now?* Yet people who approach their lives and job responsibilities with a humble heart will always involve others in their critical decisions.

All of us are smarter than one of us. Getting consistent counsel as we grow is not just smart; it's also biblical. Consider...

"A wise person will listen and continue to learn, and an understanding person will gain direction" (Proverbs 1:5, GWT).

"Where there is no guidance the people fall, but in abundance of counselors there is victory" (Proverbs 11:14, NASB).

"The way of a fool is right in his own eyes, but a wise man is he who listens to counsel" (Proverbs 12:15, NASB).

"Plans go wrong for lack of advice; many counselors bring success" (Proverbs 15:22, NLT).

OK, you get the point. We don't know it all, and if we obtain wise counsel, it may put us in a better position to obtain victory.

One specific way humble people involve others is to welcome them into the decision-making process. That's getting counsel when it's most useful—while there's still time for it to impact the direction of a ministry or life.

Here's an example of what can happen when there's a humility deficit in the decision-making process:

When General Robert E. Lee encountered Union troops near Gettysburg, Pennsylvania, he was a man accustomed to winning. A brilliant strategic thinker, Lee had been able to achieve victories while engaging far larger northern armies. He apparently didn't see any reason the conflict at Gettysburg should be any different.

On July 3, 1863, Lee ordered a frontal attack on the very center of the Union lines. It was a decision Lee's seasoned advisor, General Longstreet, urged his commander to reconsider. But Lee persisted, and thirteen thousand Confederate soldiers walked across a mile of open field, under withering fire from Union soldiers situated on higher ground. Pickett's charge, as it was later called, cost a staggering 60 percent casualty rate—and failed. Lee's men were mowed down in a hail of cannon shot and gunfire.

Imagine Lee's feelings as wounded soldiers were dragged back to his lines, as he stared out across a field littered with thousands of dead soldiers wearing Confederate gray.

Perhaps he'd thought they were invincible, that *he* was invincible.

Lee was wrong. And though the great general was beloved by his men and respected by his peers, his slight sliver of arrogance had cost him a major campaign...and an entire army.

A wise leader keeps in mind that he or she doesn't know it all—and takes this counsel to heart:

"Arrogant know-it-alls stir up discord, but wise men and women listen to each other's counsel" (Proverbs 13:10, *The Message*).

"A stubborn fool considers his own way the right one, but a person who listens to advice is wise" (Proverbs 12:15, GWT).

Humble people will...
Lift up others.

Lifting up others involves...others. I hesitate to even mention it because it's so obvious, but I've had the experience of forgetting this one myself. And I've also observed the tendency in others to act as if they're alone in the universe and their concerns are the most important thing in existence.

They don't lift up others because they don't really *notice* others.

It's easy to begin believing that your needs are above everyone else's, especially when what you need is needed to enhance ministry. Maybe it's true that you could use three more nursery workers, but I can guarantee you won't find them if you're too preoccupied to notice the seventeen workers God has already brought you.

The Bible specifically says to "think of ways to encourage one another to outbursts of love and good deeds" (Hebrews 10:24, NLT). When we're not lifting up others, we have the tendency to develop a sense of entitlement or an "I deserve to be treated in a different way because of what I have achieved" attitude.

Trust me: Humility doesn't hang out where there are feelings of entitlement because of past victories.

Want to "attain" humility? Here are two approaches. Which do you think will ultimately succeed with God's blessings?

Absorbed with themselves	**A**ware of others' needs
Taking from others	**T**rusting those around them
Thankless in their approach	**T**hankful for what they have
Apathetic in dealing with others	**A**ctive in the lives of others
Immature in their dealings	**I**nvolved in the interests of others
Navigating their own lives	**N**egotiating for others

Humble people will...
Increase in God's power and decrease in their own.

Here are some great ways to identify prideful people. They care deeply about titles and indications of power.

Prideful people are more concerned about who has the title, the biggest office, and the thickest carpet than about actually getting the job done. And that tendency isn't just on display in businesses; it's also observable in the church.

Listen, I've done enough worrying about those things for all of us. After thirteen years of children's ministry, I can honestly say that the corner office isn't all it's cracked up to be. When I started in children's ministry, they cleaned out a closet, and that was my first office. No joke—a closet.

Once I landed a full-time position, I felt I deserved more than a closet. So they moved me over to where the "regular" staff sat and walled in another corner for me. I had no windows, just four walls and a door. Everyone else had offices with windows, but not me.

As I became a bit more proficient in my ministry to children, they let me paint and wallpaper my office and even gave me a built-in bookcase. But still no window.

I stayed in that office until I was hired at Saddleback Church. One of my first questions was "Excuse me, will I have an office?"

The answer: "Absolutely."

I was escorted back to my office. And, guess what? A *window office!* Yep, there was a window in the door. It looked out into the hallway.

A room with a view...

Are you kidding me? I thought. *I deserve a real window. I've been doing this for six years!* I sat in that office for four years, until we built a new office building. Then, finally, I got it—a corner office with a window. And now I don't even look out that window very much. Why? Because I'd rather stare into the window that lets me see my staff than stare out the window that faces outside.

People make a difference. Scenery doesn't.

What does this have to do with Christ's power increasing and mine decreasing? Everything, because I've discovered that the perks and parking spots and windows don't matter. This ministry thing isn't about you and me. It's about Jesus. Who cares if we have a window? We may think that a nice office communicates respect and authority, but in the end it comes down to this: Are you making a difference?

Humble people seem to be able to have impact without a walnut desk. People like Jesus, for one.

The Scriptures below reinforce my point that it's all about God's power working in us, not about increasing our own power over the power other people leverage for influence.

"Jesus must become more important, while I become less important" (John 3:30, CEV).

"All who make themselves great will be made humble, but those who make themselves humble will be made great" (Luke 14:11).

"First pride, then the crash—the bigger the ego, the harder the fall" (Proverbs 16:18, *The Message*).

When God's power increases in our lives, we become less consumed with looking out windows or even with how we're treated. Humble people are some of the most secure, least political people I know. Why? Because they're doing what they know God has called them to do, and they're aiming to hear, "Well done, good and faithful servant." They don't care for a moment if they ever hear, "Your reserved parking spot is next to the door."

Humble people will...
Thank others.

I've briefly mentioned this before, but let me expand on it here. People whose character is predominantly arrogant and prideful feel they have a sense of entitlement. And along with entitlement comes an unwillingness to be thankful.

Consider Jesus' healing of the lepers:

"While He was on the way to Jerusalem, He was passing between Samaria and Galilee. As He entered a village, ten leprous men who stood at a distance met Him; and they raised their voices, saying, 'Jesus, Master, have mercy on us!'

"When He saw them, He said to them, 'Go and show yourselves to the priests.' And as they were going, they were cleansed.

"Now one of them, when he saw that he had been healed, turned back, glorifying God with a loud voice, and he fell on his face at His feet, giving thanks to Him. And he was a Samaritan.

"Then Jesus answered and said, 'Were there not ten cleansed? But the nine— where are they? Was no one found who returned to give glory to God, except this foreigner?'

"And He said to him, 'Stand up and go; your faith has made you well'" (Luke 17:11-19, NASB).

Why did one turn back and say thank you, while nine others kept going down the road?

Well, nine felt entitled, and one did not. I hope you don't take this as too much of an overstatement, but I have found that this story serves as a pretty consistent percentage in the church, as well. Often I see 90 percent moving on while only 10 percent return to say thank you.

We need to be thankful for everything we have. Corrie ten Boom was thankful for the lice that had infested the barracks of the Nazi prison camp where she and others were being held. Why? Because most of the Nazi guards wouldn't come into their barracks due to the infestation. It seems there is always *something* to be thankful for, if we can just let go of our conceit and pride long enough to see it.

And if conceit and pride seem like a fine thing, think again:

"There is one thing worse than a fool, and that is a man who is conceited" (Proverbs 26:12, *TLB*).

Humble people will...
Yield their power to Christ's power.

OK, we know that all our gifts and power flow from Christ. But even knowing that, we often look to our own strengths when we do things that are within our gift mix.

We don't surrender as much or go to our knees as quickly when we feel we can "pull it off" on our own. We forget about the dangers associated with such behavior: We become overconfident, and we let our pride and ego get in the way.

In August 1969, a group of people on the Gulf Coast of Mississippi learned first-hand the dangers of such overconfidence. For this to make any sense at all, you have to first understand what a "hurricane party" is. We don't have them in California, and I'm betting if you live in Oklahoma, you haven't attended one lately, either.

The idea behind a hurricane party is to wait until your area is being evacuated in the face of a coming hurricane. Then, when the final call to evacuate comes, you don't leave. Instead, you board up the windows, buy extra chips and dip, and invite other people who won't evacuate to hunker down with you to wait out the storm.

The guest of honor at this particular party on the Gulf Coast was a storm named Camille, and the party was held in the Richelieu Apartments in Pass Christian, Mississippi. The stately complex stood right on the coast, so the twenty-four party guests enjoyed front-row seats as Camille churned and howled ever nearer.

Camille's wrath intensified just before she hit the coast. Winds of over two hundred miles per hour battered the walls of the Richelieu Apartments. A storm surge wave of twenty-four feet slammed into the building, literally washing it away.

One of the women attending the party survived, but she was washed more than twelve miles inland. The rest of those ill-fated merrymakers—all of whom knew what might happen—had attended their last party on earth.

They thought they could handle the storm. They were wrong.

Perspective Is the Answer

One of my professors in college, Dr. Radcliffe, had a great sense of wit and humor. He would occasionally poke a little fun at a student who appeared to have it all together or appeared a bit too high on himself.

I was apparently one of those students. He'd say, "I would like to introduce you to Craig; he wrote the book *Humility, and How I Attained It*."

It's not ironic that this particular chapter on pride and humility appears in the center of this book on essentials for healthy leaders in children's ministry. I'm learning that through life and through our spiritual journey, the first six themes of this book and the next five themes are all connected to this chapter's theme.

Why can't we say that all of us are smarter than one of us? Because our ego won't let us.

Why don't we make right choices? Because we are arrogant.

Why can't we lead from the inside out? Because we are full of pride.

Why can't we control the flow? Because we like to be in the center of it all.

The essence of failure is pride, arrogance, and ego.

The bottom line is that a humble person is not someone who thinks he's nothing. A humble person knows he *is* something, but he recognizes God as the source of his greatness. Thinking one is something without recognizing God as the source leads to arrogance. Here is how the Scriptures put it...

· *Humble people realize who God really is.*

"So he said to me, 'This is the word of the Lord to Zerubbabel: "Not by might nor by power, but by my Spirit," says the Lord Almighty' " (Zechariah 4:6, NIV).

· *Humble people realize who they really are.*

"We are like clay jars in which this treasure is stored. The real power comes from God and not from us" (2 Corinthians 4:7, CEV).

Even God himself didn't blast onto the earthly scene dressed in the finest new baby gear. Nor was he born in the best hospital in town.

No, he chose a humble stable, not even a room in the inn. He chose not a bed but a trough. I don't know of a more humble way to enter the world nor a more humble way to leave it than the way Jesus did.

God incarnate emptied himself, taking the form of a servant and being made in the likeness of man. Yet the ultimate result of this humility was the highest exultation, forever (see Philippians 2:9-11).

Even if I could believe that I had completely overcome arrogance, I would probably be proud of my humility and how I attained it. That's how hopeless I am apart from the grace of God.

How is it with you?

Dive In! (Questions for Reflection and Discussion)

I. Who is the humblest person you've ever known? Name some of his or her qualities and actions.

2. Where are you on the humility scale? How can you tell?

3. Pick one of the eight qualities of a humble person, and share an example demonstrating your *growth* in that area.

4. Pick one of the eight qualities of a humble person, and share an example demonstrating your *need* for growth in that area.

5. In your small group, talk about how strong, healthy leadership goes together with humility. Use practical examples to illustrate your points.

DIVING RULES AND TOOLS

Tool: *Wet suit*

Spiritual Application:
Your wet suit protects you from cold water, its thick insulation designed to keep you warm for hours. The Bible reminds us that we are *in* the world but not *of* the world. We need a layer of insulation to protect us from the cold temperatures that arrogance can produce in us.

The reminder for all of us is to "suit up" as we enter the waters of ministry. If we don't wear a wet suit on a cold-water dive, it will be, at the very least, unpleasant—at the very worst, fatal.

Notes

I. Find the quotation by William Temple at this Web site: http://allthingswilliam.com/humility.html

Chapter 8

The Big Balancing Act: Communication

Growing in vulnerability to God—and other people—requires growing communication skills.

Dive Rule: *Learn to communicate underwater.*

Communication is critical in scuba diving. Sometimes you have to communicate to stay alive. If you run out of air at eighty feet, you're in big trouble—unless you have a buddy next to you who'll share the air and take you to the top. Learn to communicate at eighty feet, and you'll have no problem at the surface.

Recently I was pulled over and awarded a "gift certificate" from my friends at the California Highway Patrol. I'm on a first-name basis with those particular friends, and I've learned some valuable lessons from them about communication.

The first time I was pulled over, I was over-the-top nice and pleasant. Yes, Officer; no, Officer; on my best behavior. I presented my driver's license in the proper manner, and my timing was impeccable. Hands on the steering wheel, in full view, so as to not "scare" the officer. I provided my proof of insurance and registration with precision and poise. I answered the officer's direct questions with direct responses.

Bottom line, I got a ticket. A pretty big one, too.

The second time I got pulled over, I was a little slower at producing my documentation. I was cordial but not over-the-top nice. I created some casual conversation and...still got a gift certificate. A pretty expensive one, too.

The next time I was pulled over (three times in three months!), as the officer approached my car, I curtly asked, "Can you just write the gift certificate quickly? Here's my license, registration, and proof of insurance. I'm in a hurry; I was wrong; I blew it. Just whatever you do, do it quickly."

You know, I still got a gift certificate, but the process took twice as long. At the end of our little "time together," the officer informed me that he had been planning to just give me a warning. But then, because of the way I approached the conversation, I earned the gift certificate instead.

Meaningful, caring dialogue could have made such a difference.

Have you ever made a similar mistake?

If I had just let him speak first. But, no, I had to open my mouth and insert not only my foot but everything else, too.

I was so sure I knew what he thought about that issue. If I'd just checked my assumptions before I went after him at the meeting.

That guy is so touchy. Who knew he'd get offended by an innocent joke like that?

I've said exactly the wrong thing not only to my friends in the California Highway Patrol but also with church friends. In front of committees. With teachers, leaders, and bosses. And, now that I think about it, with about any other group I can recall.

Sometimes I've tried to second-guess a situation and used the wrong language or perhaps miscommunicated my intent or vision. I've even tried to "politic" my agenda to win a conversational debate.

I know that great decisions come from receiving all relevant information and laying it all out on the table before arriving at a conclusion. Yet, too many times, I've simply slapped my own ideas down on the table and decided that's all the information I need to consider.

I've been on the other end of a communication missile too. Several years ago I was verbally wounded by someone during a group discussion. At first I thought I was being oversensitive. Then I did a little processing and realized that sensitivity is *not* one of my strong points, and I was still bleeding from the words. Whoever coined the phrase "sticks and stones may break my bones but names will never hurt me" never got hit with one of the hundred-pound words flying around at *that* meeting.

Getting a Communication Clue

There was a time I had no idea there was such a thing as "tactical communication." I was clueless about words such as *leverage* and *agenda* and how important those words and concepts are in communication.

But leadership—even in the church—wakes you up in a hurry to the need to get savvy in communicating!

When I first learned words like *leverage* and *agenda*, I was concerned about whether they were biblical. They felt...well, *wrong*. Like maybe when we're so intentional about our communication and its consequences, we're somehow out of line.

But here's the truth: You can't get too savvy about how you communicate and why. If you're in ministry, you're in the people business, and communication is how you connect with people.

There are heavy words and light words. I don't mean that some have fewer calories than the others, but the rate at which you speak, your inflection, your cadence, and how you craft your words give them weight. And occasionally, when they fall or get hurled—or simply dropped—they can injure beyond a simple broken bone. They can be paralyzing.

Healthy leaders know how to communicate and communicate clearly. They push through the barriers and connect with people because the cost of not connecting is simply too high.

Besides, if you wish to be vulnerable with others, that's going to happen through your communication. Even if you decide to let your actions speak for you, there will come a time you need to explain yourself.

People communicate in lots of ways. I've observed people who attempt to make their point by using verbal intimidation, crying, pouting, or an over-the-top emotional delivery. Even a good message can get lost in the delivery when someone uses the wrong method of communication.

The fact is there are rules for fair, open communication. We're called to play by them even if others ignore them.

In the first half of this chapter, we'll look closely at communication rules—five of the big ones, at least. Later I'll suggest some steps you can take should your communication processes become "ugly" and head for breakdown.

The "Big Five" Rules of Communication

I am passionate about children's ministry, and unashamedly so. That's why I sometimes find myself resorting to some terrible communication techniques in an attempt to get something for a group of kids.

I lose my cool, interrupt somebody, fail to listen, intimidate verbally, or just fire off my feelings without thinking about how my monologue will sound to others. All to push my agenda, which I, of course, think is pure and righteous.

Boy, can I be wrong.

Listen to what Scripture says regarding verbal tactics in communication:

"A wise, mature person is known for his understanding. The more pleasant his words, the more persuasive he is" (Proverbs 16:21, TEV).

In other words, I'd better *watch what I say*. You, too, by the way.

You can make or break your meeting or discussion by using the wrong language, the wrong cadence, the wrong inflection, or the wrong tone. Be kind and honoring in your conversation, even if you are being treated unfairly.

That's where the Big Five come in.

Rule #1: Remember that less is more.

Often, the less you say, the better.

James 5:12 in *The Message* says, "Since you know that he cares, let your language show it. Don't add words like 'I swear to God' to your own words. Don't show your impatience by concocting oaths to hurry up God. Just say yes or no. Just say what is true. That way, your language can't be used against you."

A friend told me the government once published a regulations manual on the sale of cabbage that totaled over 25,000 words! Now, I don't know if that's true, but it sounds possible. And if the manual was made up of average, single-spaced pages containing roughly four hundred words each, it was a sixty-two-page book on the sale of cabbage! I doubt this "novel" was a life-changer. Twenty-five thousand words and I'll bet there's not one line that carried enough emotional punch to get it quoted in a speech.

I was recently in Gettysburg, Pennsylvania, and stood where President Lincoln gave his historic address on November 19th, 1863. I just finished counting the words to his speech, and they number 267, a far cry from 25,000.

But more was said in those few hundred words than I'm sure was said in the cabbage epic. Lincoln's address was poignant, emotional, and energetic. It was a sparse speech, but one loaded with content and power.

As I stood where Lincoln stood that day, I could imagine his cadence and tone as he communicated with emotion and compassion. He certainly said more with less that day.

For fun, check the shortest verse in the Bible. It's found in John 11:35: "Jesus wept." Two tiny words—but what an amazing amount they tell us about Jesus.

When it comes to communication, it's not about the number of words you say. In fact, the more you say, the less credible you may appear to be.

In college we used to joke about the know-it-alls—always raising their hands, always acing the quizzes, always winning the debates. They were good thinkers but typically quite controlling. It wasn't that they were smart; it was how they *communicated* that they were smart. The attitude. The smugness.

We usually said something along the lines of "Just give them enough rope, and eventually they'll hang themselves." And now that I've been out of school long enough to see how those guys' lives turned out, that observation proved true.

And so has this one from Proverbs: "Those who love to talk will experience the consequences, for the tongue can kill or nourish life" (Proverbs 18:21, NLT).

Rule #2: Honor them, even if they're miserable.

The tough part about communicating with someone who doesn't care about you or what you have to offer is that you *do* have to care about them. Yes, you treat them with honor. You even admit that there is always something to learn from such folks.

God uses other people and their communication styles to refine who we are. Luke 6:27-28 (*The Message*) says, "To you who are ready for the truth, I say this: Love your enemies. Let them bring out the best in you, not the worst. When someone gives you a hard time, respond with the energies of prayer for that person."

When someone gives you a hard time, how do you respond? The New Living Translation says, "Pray for the happiness of those who curse you."

Why does God want us to pray for the happiness of those who are verbally cutting out our hearts? *Because their lives are so constantly miserable,* that's why.

It's out of the abundance of their own hearts that they speak. Can you imagine the inner turmoil that must be behind people who are so brutal (or inept) that their communication is laced with such poison? They have to live with themselves twenty-four hours a day, seven days a week, so you can put up with them for five minutes, right?

The writer of Proverbs 15 put it this way: "Every day is a terrible day for a miserable person, but a cheerful heart has a continual feast" (Proverbs 15:15, GWT).

Rule #3: Communicate in order to understand.

One of the reasons we need to hone our communication skills is that, if we don't have good abilities in this area, our interactions with others will likely fall into one of three less-than-optimum frameworks:

1. I win—you lose;
2. I want out, so I'll withdraw; or
3. I'll give in to keep things "nice."

None of these are going to help you lead effectively—or grow in vulnerability.

Someone once described communication to me by using the analogy of a teeter-totter. One side of the teeter-totter represents people whose primary way of communication is *to win*. The other side of the teeter-totter is for those whose primary way of communicating is *to have harmony*. The right way to communicate is to be balanced in our communication *and* to strive for *understanding*.

There is a balance point to communication. When you go up and down on a teeter-totter, you balance on a simple lever called a fulcrum. When you have two individuals of equal size and weight going back and forth, you have a pleasant teeter-totter experience.

If you're paired with someone not equal to you in size and weight, you experience disequilibrium. In fact, if you are the lighter of the two, you can take a very unpleasant journey up—and an even worse journey back down.

The same is true in communication. If one party in the conversation is only trying to win and the other is seeking harmony, then you're looking at a win-win situation. The winner will get his way, and the person whose primary goal is harmony will also get his way.

However, there's still disequilibrium because understanding has not been achieved. The whole relationship is still out of balance, and the harmony-seeker constantly ends up on the bottom.

All structural engineers design to what they call a *meta point*. When you design a boat, you start with the meta point. When you design a car, you start with the meta point. When you design an airplane, you start with the meta point.

A meta point is the point of balance or buoyancy. The future of the vehicle is based on balance. The same is true in communication. Find the point of balance, and proceed from there. We call that point *understanding*.

There have been times I've been at the top of that teeter-totter, and everyone on the playground was looking to see how I would handle the uncomfortable situation.

The good news is that eight direct and simple words can make the difference: *"When you say that, it makes me feel..."*

Maybe Anne has made a critical comment about your ability to effectively pull off a large event at your church. The comment was bad enough, but it was hurled at you in the context of a board meeting. Ouch.

There you are at the top of the teeter-totter. Everyone on the playground is looking at you, wondering what's going to come next. Will you fire back an equally inappropriate remark? be snide? be prideful? pretend nothing was said?

The thing is, you may want to have a dialogue with Anne about her comment. You may want to learn what's behind it and find out areas in which you can improve. And you're determined to follow the Big Five rules, even if Anne hasn't chosen to follow them.

Time to pull out your eight words and formulate them into a response. It may sound something like this...

"Wow. (Pause.) Anne, (pause) when you say that, (pause) it really makes me feel as if you don't value my contribution to the team..."

Then signal back to Anne that you want her to respond so you can enter a dialogue. Make eye contact. Speak gently.

You've used honoring language, you've treated her with dignity and respect, and you've also let her know that you don't want that type of barbed comment to come in your direction again. So together you'll work on the problem.

Try These Techniques for Better Communicating

Most of our communication problems stem from our reluctance to be direct. It's possible to state what we want and still remain gracious, respectful, and "Christlike." Then, once we have the real topic of our conversation out on the table, we can listen and reply more effectively.

How to do it? Consider:

When confronting, use "I" statements.
"I'm feeling a little hurt about..."

Restate what you hear, before you reply.
"Let me see if I'm hearing you right, Ken. You think the new VBS idea will create chaos, and you're feeling a bit uneasy about the kind of logistical challenges it'll bring..."

Practice reflecting for empathy.
"You're having some fear about the new job, then?"

Avoid dirty fighting tactics.
1. Don't use gross generalizations.
2. Don't attack the person instead of the problem.
3. Don't haul out all past grievances.
4. Don't make vague accusations.
5. Don't play one-upmanship.
6. Don't constantly question another's motives or understanding.
7. Don't sink to sarcasm.

Seek the Deep

If we were to think in terms of bringing our communication levels to the very "depths" of the ocean (that is, communicating from the depths of our hearts), we could chart things this way:

Level 1: Entering the Surf

Content: Exchanging routine information.

Example: *"Pastor, I just finished my report about last night's Kid Koncert. It's on your desk."*

"Thanks, Bill. I plan to read through it this afternoon."

Level 2: Moving Beyond the Beach

Content: Discussing events in others' lives.

Example: *"Hey, Carlos, did you hear that the Martinez family is vacationing in Switzerland this year?"*

"Really? I bet the kids will have a blast!"

Level 3: Diving Under the Waves

Content: Offering opinions and ideas.

Example: *"I think we should have separate rooms for our infants and toddlers. I've seen some of the two-year-olds throwing toys near the cribs, and I don't like that one bit."*

"Not a problem, Karissa! Hey, what if we just put a wall in right here? What do you think? Should we raise the issue at the budget meeting?"

Level 4: Swimming Down to the Depths

Content: Sharing feelings and needs.

Example: *"Sometimes I wish my mom was still around helping me out. I'm really missing her these days, especially when it comes to needing her wisdom about family life."*

"Ah! My dad passed away at a young age too. I'm feeling pretty sad during this holiday season...What was your mom like?"

Level 5: Reaching the Solid, Rocky Floor

Content: Risking complete transparency

Example: *"Hey, Bill, I have to tell you, I'm struggling with lying to my boss about how I'm spending my time. It's tearing me up; can you help?"*

"Maybe we could form an accountability team. I've experienced the same temptations at my work too. Actually, I'm glad you said something."

Rule #4: Check your feelings at the door.

Most of us feel we must "win" when we communicate.

Even if you value harmony, you seem to win as long as everyone leaves liking each other; that's your definition of *winning*.

But when you communicate for the purpose of understanding, you have to proceed with an open mind, trying to see where the other person is coming from. Winning is irrelevant; understanding the other person is what's important.

How does this apply to you, personally? Well, all of us have our passions. Mine is children's ministry. I'll push that agenda all day long; that's easy for me. You have your passions and agendas too.

But children's ministry isn't the only ministry in my church. (Before you all pick up a rock, hear me out!) There's also worship, discipleship, fellowship, and evangelism. Plus, our kids have families so there are adults in the church...and teenagers. Sometimes I may not get the budget I wanted even after I've argued, begged, and pleaded.

That's OK. I can check my feelings at the door.

Maybe another ministry within the church needs the money more, so I don't get what I want. When I check my feelings at the door and focus on understanding rather than arguing to get my agenda met, I have a better chance at communicating in a win-win environment later on. I can see the other people's points and appreciate their feelings and situations.

Besides, there's always *next* budget season!

Rule #5: Use emotional word pictures.

I was driving down the Pennsylvania turnpike when I came across a team of people doing work along the shoulder of the road. It was a typical work crew, wearing their standard, bright orange vests. And they were working diligently at their jobs.

As I slowed my car to keep a safe speed, I became frustrated. I was already running several minutes late, and I was in unfamiliar territory.

Part of me was watching the road, another part was on the phone trying to get directions, yet another part was trying to find where I was on a map, and the last sliver of me was watching the people doing the roadwork.

As the traffic slowed to a crawl, I became more irritated. *These people are making me late. Couldn't they have done this roadwork during the evening?*

And just as I reached the pinnacle of my selfishness, I saw a road sign that changed my perspective. In fact, the sign changed my life.

It was an ordinary sign, but the words on it were overwhelmingly powerful. The sign was the standard orange sign that would normally read, "Slow, men at work." But instead of those words, it said, "Please slow down. My daddy works here!"

Another sign said, "Please slow down. My mommy works here!"

Wow! Frustration drained from my body. I hung up the phone, put down the map, and focused on avoiding hitting the people working around me. Why?

Because someone's parents were working there. The message had been communicated in a powerful image.

This week, as you talk with your family and friends, choose your words carefully. Occasionally use words that express emotion and create a mental image.

When you connect with people's emotions, your message becomes far more memorable than if you just string words together. People don't think about delays when they see a sign about Mommy and Daddy. No, they think about little Samantha with her big brown eyes, pleading with you to take care of her loved one.

Images like that can cause people to change their behavior...at least, I did. Images like that can crystallize a vision for your ministry—and communicate it clearly and powerfully.

When Communication Gets Ugly

Occasionally communication can be harsh. This past Sunday after I finished preaching here at Saddleback, I was standing outside talking to one of the folks who had attended the service. That's when I noticed a little boy about six years old who had been standing next to me for the longest time.

I turned to him and asked where his parents were. He told me they were talking to some friends and then pointed them out. Then, without hesitation, the little boy reached into his pocket and pulled out two quarters and handed them to me.

"What are these for?" I asked.

"Daddy said you're one of the poorest speakers he ever heard," said the boy. "I just wanted to help you out."

Ouch!

It's not only the actual words we speak that make up our communication. It's also our tone and body language. Even silence can scream when you see it being used to wound another person.

Can I suggest something that you probably already know? There's some unhealthy communication evidenced in the church. There are people who use their position and power to wound others. Is it intentional? I don't know, but I do know this: Wounded people wound other people.

I've seen hallway conversations in which it was suggested that a person consider a new way of teaching a class turn into battles. Ugly words were hurled—and I suspect that they came from a hurting heart. What we say and how we say it are direct reflections of what's inside us.

Communication patterns are usually deeply engrained in people. It takes years to learn the bad habits, and learning to replace them with healthy ways to communicate won't happen overnight. If you have a person or people in your ministry circle who use communication as a weapon, pray for those folks. And protect yourself with appropriate boundaries, as you continue to seek balanced communication.

Here are some practical steps you can take that are both biblical and effective when it comes to communicating with others.

What the Bible Says About Our Communication

Honor others with what you say.
"Don't bad-mouth each other, friends. It's God's Word, his Message, his Royal Rule, that takes a beating in that kind of talk. You're supposed to be honoring the Message, not writing graffiti all over it" (James 4:11, *The Message*).

Picture those you're talking about as sitting right next to you.
"A devious person spreads quarrels. A gossip separates the closest of friends" (Proverbs 16:28, GWT).

Practice saying less.
"A gossip tells secrets, so don't hang around with someone who talks too much" (Proverbs 20:19, NLT).

Be patient with the most difficult people.
"The Lord's servants must not quarrel but must be kind to everyone. They must be able to teach effectively and be patient with difficult people. They should gently teach those who oppose the truth. Perhaps God will change those people's hearts, and they will believe the truth" (2 Timothy 2:24-25, NLT).

Step I: Show up.
The first step in healthy communication is simply to show up.

Maybe you think this is no big deal, but it's huge. For those who have tumbled under the heavy rocks of a violent communicator, you know what I'm talking about. It's often easier to walk away or "take" verbal punishment than to show up and weather the storm.

Showing up means engaging. It means letting a verbal bully know that his or her words are heard and received—and they sting.

This is the first step and one of the toughest.

Step 2: Quiet up.
Be silent before God and the person with whom you're communicating. Clear your mind. Look into his or her eyes. Give the person your entire, focused attention.

Several years ago I worked for a person who had a dominant style of communicating. In fact, he was on a rant with me while I was sat in his office. I'd "shown up" but I wasn't about to "quiet up." Why? Because I was also trying to control the conversation.

So what did I do as the barrage continued to get louder and more forceful? I simply sunk lower in the chair, disengaged eye contact, yawned, periodically glanced at my watch, and generally did everything I could nonverbally to let him know that I could not be controlled, nor could I be more disinterested in what he was saying.

Who was wrong in this situation?

We both were.

We generally think of people who are controlling communicators as being loud and boisterous, but that's not always the case. I was being just as controlling as the other person; I was just being quiet about it.

Occasionally we receive news we don't want to hear. Perhaps it's about a leader, our budget, a new program, or a child in the program. We tense up on the inside. We start to formulate a response before we get all the facts. Emotions run high, and we jump in to attack before we have all the data.

We need to quiet up. Quieting up is not about volume; it's about focus and maintaining a calm spirit. It's about seeking understanding.

Step 3: Listen up.

After you show up, and quiet up, it's time to listen up. It must be difficult to listen, or the Bible wouldn't give so much advice on it. We are reminded in the book of James: "My dear brothers and sisters, always be willing to listen and slow to speak. Do not become angry easily, because anger will not help you live the right kind of life God wants" (James 1:19-20).

Maybe you've noticed that we've been given two ears and one mouth. Do the math: It's at least a two-to-one trade-off.

Have you ever been in a conversation with somebody who keeps finishing your sentences for you? These are people who typically dominate on the playground but lose in the boardroom.

There are times I'm not listening very well, and those are the times I will take out my pen and paper and write down what the person is saying to me. For me, this is critical because it links to the next step.

If you are not listening intently, you won't hear the other person's *heart* on the matter, or even his or her complete view. Often my wife will say, "You are not hearing me correctly." Most of the time, this is true because while she's talking I'm trying to formulate my response. Focused listening builds understanding.

Step 4: Follow up.

After showing up, quieting up, and listening up, it's time to follow up. The six most important words you can say to help accomplish this are "What I hear you saying is..."

Around our children's ministry, you hear those words a lot. It's almost a joke. After I give some vision or direction to one of my team members, that person may say, as he or she looks at a note pad, "What I hear you saying is..." and then repeat what the person "thought" he or she heard me say.

And it works both ways. When one of my staff communicates to me, at the end of the dialogue I'll often say, "What I hear you saying is..."

The reason for this follow-up step is to make sure we're all on the same page. In our haste we often confuse delivering a monologue that has no question and answer period with actually communicating. They're not the same. We can't expect to deliver a speech and have the receivers listen, comprehend, and then apply what we've just told them.

Dialogue is a two-way street. We must provide appropriate feedback to make sure we've heard what the other person is really saying, and we must allow others to check with us about our communication, too.

Step 5: Grow up.

OK, all of the information has been presented, and you didn't get your way. This is the final step in balanced communication, and here are three words for you: *Get over it.* We all need to grow up occasionally when our feelings are hurt because we didn't get our way.

If you don't get over it, you'll fall into one of my three favorite groups in the church: the whiners, the criers, and the complainers. Honestly, I can hardly stand to talk with any of them. I don't know how else to say it. If you're a whiner, crier, or complainer, you probably won't like what I'm about to say. If you're *not* a whiner, crier, or complainer, get out your highlighter—you need to remember this stuff.

Whiners, criers, and complainers are people who are purely excuse-oriented. It's always someone else's fault that they couldn't meet the deadline or get the job done.

If this is your style of communication, get over it. Move on. It's not somebody else's fault; it's your fault.

Our senior pastor says God is more concerned about your character than your comfort. Maybe the communication at hand isn't about you. Maybe it's about what God is doing *in* you.

I think we all enjoy getting our way occasionally. However, we all need to grow up and accept that it's a blessing when our team reaches a conclusion—even if it isn't our favorite conclusion. We can all rejoice together because it was probably the right conclusion.

In any case, you can't have balanced communication unless you're willing to relinquish your agenda to the overall agenda of heaven—what God wants to do *in* your life and *through* your life. And that requires a daily commitment to growing up in Christ.

There are many ways to communicate, but I believe there are three major approaches. Which one sounds most like you?

The Violent Communicator

Violent communication doesn't always take the form of screaming or raised voices. Sometimes a violent communicator takes the form of the...

Intimidator:
This person communicates in ways that are dishonoring, devaluing, and humiliating. Talk with an Intimidator, and you'll get the feeling that you've done something wrong or you *intend* to do something wrong.

Occasionally commanding in language, and often very articulate, Intimidators push their agendas. And while the agendas may be right, there's damage done to people with whom Intimidators communicate as they pursue getting their way.

Dictator:
With this person it's "my way or the highway." Enough said.

Debater:
Communicating with this person is like nailing Jell-O to the wall; it just won't stick. Sometimes deliberately vague, sometimes delivering information in monstrous detail (remember the 25,000-word volume on cabbage sales), the Debater always has a perfectly good reason for doing or saying whatever was done or said...and is prepared to debate the rationale.

If you feel unable to participate in any meaningful dialogue with a Debater, that's no accident. It's how the person wins and gets his or her way.

Instigator:
The Instigator likes to create disharmony. If you're in ministry, you think of it as "They enjoy a good debate." If you're not in ministry, you think, "They really enjoy a good fight."

Instigators are at their best when toe-to-toe with the opposition. They process information quickly and prey on those who process more slowly. They're typically very good with words and fast on their feet. They get their way but don't leave many other people standing after they've gone to war.

A biblical reminder for those who embrace the Violent Way:
"Don't walk around with a chip on your shoulder, always spoiling for a fight" (Proverbs 3.30, *The Message*).

The Harmonious Communicator

This communicator wants peace at any price. And if not authentic peace, at least silence and a pasted-on smile from all participants in a conflict. Sometimes a harmonious communicator takes the form of the...

Impersonator:
This person may feel like responding on the inside but won't let it out. He impersonates the relaxed-and-calm guy so he can keep things harmonious among participants. You can tell there's something he wishes he could say, but no amount of prying can drag it out of him. Unfortunately, since he's not really satisfied with the outcome, he may sabotage it later.

Investigator:
This person must find out every fact before making a decision. Yes, this is wise; however, in this case, the person is merely seeking harmony by delaying a decision.

Rationalizer:
Persons using this style will rationalize to the lowest common denominator. They can't make a decision, but they're great talkers. In fact, they can talk forever...and say nothing.

They bring harmony by never making a decision or declaring a position. They want to sit in the front of the plane, sit in the back of church, and stay in the middle of the road.

A biblical reminder for those who embrace the Harmony Way:
"Keep vigilant watch over your heart; *that's* where life starts. Don't talk out of both sides of your mouth; avoid careless banter, white lies, and gossip" (Proverbs 4:23-24, *The Message*).

The Understanding Communicator

This communicator seeks first to understand but also wants to be understood. The healthiest of the three communication styles, this is also the most difficult.

An understanding communicator may take the form of the...

Comprehender:
This person seeks to understand other people's agendas and may ask probing questions to get at what's behind a decision or a position.

Appreciator:
They value the importance of others and their styles of communication. Although they may not agree with the tactics or style, they recognize that God can use anyone for his glory.

Recognizer:
This person recognizes others' contributions to the topic under discussion. Although they may not agree with the content, they honor everyone's viewpoint and recognize the value of each person's input.

Empathizer:
People employing this style are able to connect and understand the feelings that accompany communication. They accept people for who and what they are and don't take comments personally. People who deal with an Empathizer may not get what they want, but they'll feel understood.

A biblical reminder for those who embrace the Understanding Way:
"My dear brothers and sisters, always be willing to listen and slow to speak" (James 1:19).

Dive In! (Questions for Reflection and Discussion)

I. When did you receive your last speeding ticket? How did you handle your conversation with the police officer? What did you learn?

2. Of the Big Five rules of communication, which is the easiest and which is the most difficult for you to practice consistently in your ministry? Why?

3. What is typically your goal in a conversation that occurs in the midst of conflict? Are you pleased with your usual kinds of response?

4. When does the communication tend to "get ugly" in your life? What plans do you have to prepare yourself for the next ugly event?

5. In your group, share your favorite Scriptures related to communication. Talk about how you can apply them to practical ministry situations.

DIVING RULES AND TOOLS

Rule: *Learn to communicate underwater.*

Spiritual Application:
Communication is critical in scuba diving. Sometimes your staying alive depends on it. If you run out of air at eighty feet, you're in big trouble unless you have a buddy next to you who has as an alternate air source that will take you to the top. And if you're out of air at eighty feet, your communication may take the form of grabbing, flailing, or doing whatever else you need to do to get someone else's attention.

It can be like that in meetings, too. When someone's out of air and pushed into a corner, he or she sometimes comes out swinging. Why? Because wounded people wound people, and they feel they have nothing to lose.

Stay calm and let those people breathe. If they have to live with themselves 24/7, then you can put up with them for five minutes. Learn to communicate at eighty feet, and you'll have no problem at the surface.

Chapter 9

When Hope Is All You Have

When you grow in healthy leadership, you experience challenges that can leave you feeling hopeless. Don't let yourself drown in self-pity or indecision. Seek hope.

Dive Tool: *BCD (Buoyancy Control Device)*

There are two parts to a BCD: lead weights and air. You need life's pain (the weights) and God's purpose (the fresh air of his Word and will) to attain neutral buoyancy in life.

Let me tell you about a canary you can meet if you visit the Western Mining and Railroad Museum in Helper, Utah. I don't know the canary's name, and I doubt he'd come if you called him; he appears to be long gone (and stuffed). He's sitting in a cage, on display.

This canary had an important job a hundred years ago. Miners carried caged canaries down into the coal mines with them. Not for the singing, though. Not because the canaries were prized pets. The canaries went down into the earth so miners could see whether or not the birds would die. If deadly gases were trapped in the rock, canaries would be the first to drop. If a miner saw a canary keel over, it was definitely time to head for the surface.

Quite a job, huh? The canaries had no control over their situations. One minute they're hopping around in a cage under the bright Utah sky, and the next they're hauled underground where anxious-looking men prod them to see if they're still kicking.

And if something noxious does happen, there's no way the canaries could see it coming or get out of the way. They couldn't even quit.

Ever feel like that? Like a canary in a coal mine? One minute you're fine, and the next you're hauled somewhere you don't want to go. Hope turns into hopelessness in the blink of an eye.

A traffic accident. A sudden illness. The loss of a loved one. A rebellious child. One moment you're under bright skies; the next you're in darkness.

So what does hope mean to you?

It depends a lot on your circumstances doesn't it? For example:

If you were going down in the ocean for the third time, maybe a life preserver would be a symbol of hope for you.

If you were in a burning house, maybe a fire hose would be a symbol of hope for you.

If your car were broken down on the side of the road, maybe a tow truck would be a symbol of hope for you.

I remember "having a bad day" as a youngster. But if it was on a Friday, then I'd always look forward to the "Friday surprise." I knew that every Friday my dad brought home a little present for me. If I went to bed early and Dad wasn't home yet, I'd wake up early because I knew with confidence there was a surprise waiting for me. Dad had promised. It was certain; it was guaranteed.

What is guaranteed these days for you? Is it the things you know you have the power to earn? Do you rely on the popular saying, "God helps those who help themselves"?

But, in fact, he doesn't. God helps the *hopeless.* And there are times in each of our lives we come face to face with hopelessness. When that happens, how should we respond? With H.O.P.E., of course!

Under each of the four letters in the following acrostic of H-O-P-E, we'll look at the *meaning* and then consider a related *action* to take.

And a quick explanation for why this is worth doing at all: Because if you want to connect with people and lead through difficult times, being hopeless won't help you. Nobody follows people who throw up their hands and say, "I give up! It's hopeless!"

You'll know you're growing as a leader when you can look at "hopeless situations" and see them as they are—opportunities for God to show his power.

Honor God's plans for your future.

I believe there are two types of hope.

The first is an *unsure* hope or a wish. A hope that your life will go well and that circumstances will work out. This clearly isn't the sort of hope that offers much consolation when your budget is due, the pastor has announced you're adding another church service (and complete CE program), and your child is sick.

The second hope is a *sure* hope, a hope in the character of Christ. It doesn't depend on circumstances because it's bigger than circumstance. It's not a wish but a way. It's a confident assurance in a person who promises to secure your future.

That doesn't mean your life will be predictable, but you can be assured that God has your best interests in mind. It's the kind of hope the Bible connects to faith, as seen in Hebrews 11:1 (NLT):"What is faith? It is the confident assurance that what we hope for is going to happen. It is the evidence of things we cannot yet see."

Can we know the future? No, the future isn't predictable. Nothing prepared me for what happened just over six years ago when children entered my life. My wife, Mary, and I sat staring at each other across the living room at 1 a.m., with our brand-new twins. We had just arrived home from the hospital, and I said, after a long silence, "Now what?"

I wasn't qualified to raise children. I'd never changed a diaper. I thought the weight limit printed on the side of the Huggies package referred to the amount of "material" it could hold.

I couldn't predict the future events that would transpire in my new family, but I *could* predict—because of God's promises—exactly how God would respond to me in the midst of seemingly hopeless situations. He will always respond with love, even in his silence or apparent absence.

I believe God allows unpredictable events into our lives because he is more concerned with our character than our comfort. That's why the Scripture speaks about assurance in the future because of the One who holds our future.

"I know the plans that I have for you, declares the Lord. They are plans for peace and not disaster, plans to give you a future filled with hope" (Jeremiah 29:11, GWT).

"Those who hope in the Lord will renew their strength. They will soar on wings like eagles; they will run and not grow weary, they will walk and not be faint" (Isaiah 40:31, NIV).

It's reassuring to me that God has plans for me. That gives me hope! What does it mean to have a hopeful future? Ask my kids that question and they'll say a hopeful future for them would be my promise to take them to watch fireworks. Your answer to the question may vary a bit, but you can rely on God and what he has promised. Your life is not hopeless. Your ministry is not hopeless.

As you grow in your leadership, there's a strong need to be hopeful. You must be hopeful to lead effectively, and you must be hopeful to be faithful in following God's plan for your life.

Our action of hope when we're going through difficult circumstances is to *keep trusting.*

Action: Keep trusting.

"Trust in the Lord with all your heart; do not depend on your own understanding. Seek his will in all you do, and he will direct your paths" (Proverbs 3:5-6, NLT).

Sometimes honoring God's plan for you—and trusting—means reaching out and honoring God's plan for someone else as well. It may be as simple as a touch, a human touch that means hope for the hopeless. It's true that God holds the future, but it's also true that *we are called to hold one another.*

I've been doing a lot of thinking about this question: Could touch be a symbol of hope? Well, if you're untouchable, then yes, touch could be a symbol of hope. See, for instance, how Jesus dealt with a leprosy-ridden man who came to him.

"A man with leprosy came and knelt in front of Jesus, begging to be healed. 'If you want to, you can make me well again,' he said.

"Moved with pity, Jesus touched him. 'I want to,' he said. 'Be healed!' Instantly the leprosy disappeared—the man was healed" (Mark 1:40-42, NLT).

In the time of Jesus' ministry on earth, persons with leprosy were kept outside the city gates in lives of exile. They were considered unclean, and no one would touch them for fear of contracting the disease. People went out of their way to avoid lepers. The disease was considered terminal, and there was no hope. Few people trusted that there would be a cure—not the people who avoided lepers, and not the lepers themselves.

Interestingly, the word for *touch* in this verse means more than a mere brush or handshake. The word means "to fasten to, or lay hold of," like buttoning a shirt. It was more than a handshake; it was an embrace.

The most amazing thing about this miracle, in my mind, is that Jesus embraced the man.

The very next story about Jesus doing ministry, in Mark 2, shows Jesus healing a paralyzed man but never touching him. In fact, Jesus just tells the man to get up and walk. Why? Is it harder for Jesus to heal leprosy than paralysis? No. The touch had to mean something, something significant. It was a symbol of hope to the man and to everyone who reads about it. Jesus was saying, "There is no life so ruined, so ugly, so disfigured, so repulsive, so smelly that I will not touch it!"

Here's a personal question for you: What do you have in your life that you think God won't touch? Can you imagine what the leper thought when Jesus reached out to him? and what trust was required for the leper to reach back and enter into the Savior's embrace?

What a picture of hope for the broken human spirit! Jesus is willing to touch anyone, to restore hope to the hopeless. With a savior and friend like that, how could we fear for our futures? Trust your life and ministry—and your future—into Jesus' hands, then reach out to touch the lives of others.

Open yourself to opportunities for growth.

Our children's staff members know James 1:2-4 well. In fact, we really don't call anything a problem anymore. We call ministry challenges "opportunities." We get this philosophy from James 1:2 where we're called to let trouble be an opportunity for joy. The opportunity resides in the potential outcome, a hopeful outcome.

"Dear brothers and sisters, whenever trouble comes your way, let it be an opportunity for joy. For when your faith is tested, your endurance has a chance to grow. So let it grow, for when your endurance is fully developed, you will be strong in character and ready for anything" (NLT).

God is more concerned about our character than our comfort. He's more interested in our growth than our greatness. That's why difficult circumstances enter our lives. These things help us to expand our faith and to put greater trust in our heavenly Father.

I don't know about you, but when difficult circumstances come my way, I sometimes try to handle them myself rather than trusting and relying on God. I short-circuit the process. I try to control my life and the circumstances that surround me. When this happens I typically follow a well-worn pattern that ends up becoming a cycle of defeat.

Maybe you're experiencing a tough time right now. Does the cycle described below seem familiar to you?

I. Dictatorship
We try to control our circumstances and demand the outcomes we want.

2. Discouragement
We realize we *can't* control our circumstances, and we become disheartened.

3. Despair
The situation worsens, and we sink beyond discouragement into despair—a loss of hope. We feel there's no way out.

4. Despondency
If the situation continues, we may then sink beyond despair into a state of despondency.

5. Desperation
We can end up here—in a state of recklessness resulting from the loss of hope. We'll try anything to change our situation. We may display self-destructive behavior. We no longer care what happens to our ministries or ourselves.

Why not try this alternative plan: Whenever difficulty comes your way, let it be an opportunity for joy. When trials enter your life and you feel like opting out or giving up, God urges us to keep growing...including growing in dependency on him.

Action: Keep growing.
"Yes, you will suffer for a short time. But after that, God will make everything right. He will make you strong. He will support you and keep you from falling" (1 Peter 5:10a, ICB).

Opportunities for growth come in all sizes.

I recall attending a Mighty Ducks hockey game when they were playing horribly. They had skated fifty-five minutes of truly rotten hockey, taking only six shots in the first period and six in the next. The other team took twenty-five shots through two periods.

I turned to my wife, Mary, when there were about seven minutes left in the game. I said, "OK, why don't they just skate off the ice?" They had a puck go off the post earlier in the game, had missed an attempted penalty shot, and had a goal disallowed near the end of the second period. I figured they might as well raise the white flag, sulk into the locker room, and give up.

They had already died; they just hadn't fallen down yet.

Then, with about six minutes left, they caught fire, and we watched them burn. A difficult goal in traffic got the crowd to its feet. Then, with fifty seconds left in the game, they pulled their goalie to play as the extra attacker on the ice.

And—you guessed it—with thirty seconds left they scored the goal that pushed the game into overtime.

The game ended in a tie—but *why?* Why the sudden burst of passion with just a few minutes left? Why hadn't the discouraged team called it quits? The Ducks had been beaten all night. They had been humiliated out on the ice, and even their *own fans* booed them at one point during the game.

So why, after all that, did they continue to put one skate in front of the other? Because even though they didn't have any goals, they still had hope.

Proceed through your difficulties.

Several years ago one of our baby sons had to go in for some medical testing. He was diagnosed with FTT, or Failure to Thrive. He just wasn't growing.

One of the tests was an upper GI exam, and in preparation they wrapped my one-year-old boy in a towel with his arms pinned to his side. Then they strapped him onto a "papoose" board and placed him into a cylinder. They put a washcloth on his head and strapped his head down as well. He couldn't move, as if he were in a baby straightjacket.

Then they inserted a tube through his nose, down the back of his throat, and into his stomach. The goal was to inject some fluid into his stomach that would then show up on X-ray film.

Little Cameron began to cry as they pumped the fluid into his stomach and they began to turn the cylinder. The technicians were trying to get a good X-ray by moving Cameron around in the cylinder. His crying went from sobbing to hysterical screaming.

The doctors were concerned with the test, not the emotional state of my child. Every time he would roll in the cylinder, he would see his mom to his left and me to his right. His tiny little teardrops fell to the floor whenever he was upside down.

I can only imagine what was going through his little mind: *Mom and Dad are watching them torture me, and they aren't doing anything about it! They aren't helping me, even though they're clearly in a position to do so.*

After listening to twenty minutes of screaming, I noticed that some of the fluid was coming back up through his tube and was actually leaking into his eye. I told the doctor, but he just put up his hand; he didn't want to stop looking at the screen. I tried repeatedly to get the doctor's attention, but I was met with a shrug and a hand of resistance.

Finally, I'd had enough. I spoke, at a significant volume, and said, "Everybody, this test is *over!*"

I gently encouraged the doctor with my arm to move out of the way, and then I tended to the needs of my son. Once all was well, we continued the test and found the cause of my son's condition.

Have you ever felt as if you were spinning in a cylinder of pain or difficulty with your arms strapped to your sides? Every once in a while, you get a glimpse of your heavenly Father and you say, "Why? Why don't you stop this? Why don't you help, Father?"

I could have stopped the test that day, and, in fact, for awhile that's exactly what I did. But I let it start again. Why? Because if I had stopped the test forever, we would never have known the cause of my son's problem and rid him of his Failure to Thrive.

There's a very real truth for all of us here: God will not let us out of the cylinder merely because we're crying. As a father I can tell you that our heavenly Father feels pain when we're in pain. I was crying harder than my son during the test.

Rest assured that your heavenly Father is crying right along with you and that he knows your pain. However, he won't stop the test. Doing so would deprive you of an opportunity to make you well, to grow your leadership, to deepen your skills and dependence on him.

He loves you too much for that.

Action: Hang tough.

There's an old saying: "When the going gets tough, the tough get going."

I don't know about you, but when the going gets tough, I usually feel like getting away, not getting going.

My son was in a tough situation, but that didn't make him tough enough to just gut it out. He needed help from his father—but he *also* needed to take the test. The cost of simply running away was too high to pay. There were things we needed to know about Cameron, and that terrible, uncomfortable test was the only way to get the information.

Cameron needed to hang tough—to endure the test.

Here's a passage I wish I could have shared with my one-year-old son. He couldn't have understood it, but you certainly can. It's as if Paul were writing directly to us children's ministry leaders!

"We have troubles all around us, but we are not defeated. We do not know what to do, but we do not give up the hope of living. We are persecuted, but God does not leave us. We are hurt sometimes, but we are not destroyed" (2 Corinthians 4:8-9).

Four key phrases jump out at me from that passage...

Troubles: This word refers to pressure from circumstances or antagonism from people. The word literally means "squeezed or pressed." Circumstances beyond our control can squeeze us until hope is just a memory.

Not know: The original Greek word literally means "without a way." The idea communicated is being without resources, with no place to turn. That's not an unknown feeling in leadership.

Persecuted: This can mean being pursued, to be set to flight, or to be driven away by someone.

Hurt: This word carries with it the idea of something coming at you—and you can't get away from it.

If you're in leadership, you'll deal with troubles, not knowing, persecution, and hurt. And as you proceed through your difficulties, know that God understands your situation. He has been there, and he wants to lift and love you through it.

Hang tough. You're not alone.

"For our high priest is able to understand our weaknesses. When he lived on earth, he was tempted in every way that we are, but he did not sin. Let us, then, feel very sure that we can come before God's throne where there is grace. There we can receive mercy and grace to help us when we need it" (Hebrews 4:15-16).

Expect God to uphold you.

Regardless of what's coming your way, God can help you through it.

When I played baseball in college, we had regular workouts designed to help increase our strength. Every day we were in the weight room, lifting. The bench press was a regular lift for all of us. We would start with lighter weights and then move up to the heavier lifts.

You'd always have a spotter in case you couldn't complete the lift. The spotter would remove the weight from your chest, if necessary, because you always tried to lift more than you could. That's the only way you got stronger.

God understands the idea of being your spotter.

"So don't worry, because I am with you. Don't be afraid, because I am your God. I will make you strong and will help you. I will support you with my right hand that saves you" (Isaiah 41:10, ICB).

I guess you could say that heavier-than-you-can-lift barbell might be labeled "Life." All the various weights you can bolt onto that barbell might represent various trials or difficulties in your daily existence.

Here's how the various weights might look:

1. The Mighty Ducks lost. (2.5 lbs)
2. No Dreyer's mint chocolate chip ice cream at the grocery store. (2.5 lbs)
These are easily lifted. Difficulties? Sure, but not unliftable.
3. I didn't get what I wanted for my birthday (or I had another birthday). (5 lbs)
4. The twenty-four-hour flu. (5 lbs)
5. The forty-eight-hour flu. (10 lbs)
6. My car is in the shop—again. (10 lbs)
Liftable? Probably. But when you start adding the previous weights, it gets strenuous.
7. I lost my job. (25 lbs)
8. We are having financial problems. (25 lbs)
9. I lost a long-term, supportive relationship. (35 lbs)
10. Our son ran away from home. (35 lbs)
Wow! So much weight has been added that you're struggling to lift. You'll need help to get this load off your chest.
11. I suffered abuse as a child. (45 lbs)
12. My close friend was tragically killed. (45 lbs)
13. My wife has cancer. (45 lbs)
14. My husband left me. (45 lbs)

The weight of these last four can cause you to collapse under the stress and strain of the pressure. The pain and heaviness of life have overtaken you. What will you do? Where will you turn?

Turn to God. In prayer. In worship. In a heart cry for help.

Action: Keep listening.

Are you listening right now? Here is what the Lord is saying to you:

"Come to me, all who are tired from carrying heavy loads, and I will give you rest" (Matthew 11:28, GWT).

Friends, I cannot tell you what the future holds, but I can tell you who holds your future and he says, "Give all your worries and cares to God, for he cares about what happens to you" (I Peter 5:7, NLT).

Look for God's help, delivered through his people or your circumstances or your faithful expectations. And the help you get may overwhelm you.

There's an urban legend that illustrates this point. It seems that on a cold February day, a limousine traveling down the New Jersey expressway got a flat tire. The driver climbed out to change the tire, only to discover that the spare was flat as well. Before he could summon road service, a man in a pickup truck stopped and offered to help. Among the pieces of equipment on his truck was an air tank.

As the truck driver finished up, one of the limo's windows slid down and revealed Donald Trump sitting inside. "It was very nice of you to stop and help," Trump said. "What can I do to thank you?"

The man thought for a moment and then said, "Tomorrow is Valentine's Day. My wife would really get a kick out of receiving a dozen roses from you." Trump agreed, the man jotted down his address for Trump, and the limo slid back into traffic and headed toward New York.

The next day, a messenger arrived with a box. Inside were two dozen roses and a note:

Happy Valentine's Day from a friend of your husband.
(signed) Donald Trump
P.S. Thanks for helping us out.
P.P.S. By the way, I paid off your mortgage.

Sometimes we're just hoping for a dozen roses. God wants to pay off our mortgage.

Dive In! (Questions for Reflection and Discussion)

1. When has it been the hardest for you to honor God's plans for your future? Why?

2. What opportunities for growth seem to be opening up ahead of you? What is the role of hope as you decide what to do?

3. Do you agree that God loves you, even when you're "in the cylinder"? What can others do to best comfort you and provide hope at these times? What does your response tell you about the nature of ministry?

4. When have you been certain that God was upholding you? How strong is your expectation that he will do so in the future, too?

5. How would you describe your spiritual buoyancy these days? Are you positive, negative, or neutral? What recent event gives you the best clue?

DIVING RULES AND TOOLS

Tool: BCD *(Buoyancy Control Device)*

Spiritual Application:

A BCD helps you maintain neutral buoyancy in the water. If you have *negative* buoyancy, you'll sink to the bottom—not good. Occasionally life's difficulties weigh us down, and only God's purpose for our lives will give us the buoyancy of hope we need.

But if you have *positive* buoyancy, it's also not good. You'll continue to float on top of the water and never be able to dive deep.

The BCD makes it possible for us to gain *neutral* buoyancy and become "weightless," allowing us to move freely and expend less energy in the water.

Life's painful experiences allow us to be more effective at empathizing with others. Both life's painful experiences and the hope God provides allow us to move freely to help and minister to others.

We cannot achieve neutral spiritual buoyancy without the weight of difficulty *and* the lift of God's Word. We can dive deeper only when both are present in our lives.

Part IV: Exaltation
(Spiritual Growth)
...and he pleased God. (Luke 2:52d)

Chapter 10

Oh, Be Quiet!

Spiritual growth requires you to spend time with God—focused time with God. That happens in a powerful way when you make room for solitude and silence in your life.

Dive Tool: *Dive log*

A diver's log is a record of the diver's past dives at various depths, locations, and environments. In our spiritual journey, journaling is a great way to track how spiritually "deep" we're moving. Record your explorations with your heavenly Father!

When Chuck Yeager broke the sound barrier on October 14, 1947, he was the first human to travel that fast. His flight was dubbed "the flight heard around the world." It was so named because of the tremendous sonic boom that thundered across the landscape beneath the plane's flight path. What speed! Yeager was traveling at Mach one—the speed of sound, which is about 660 miles per hour at twenty thousand feet.[1]

In the past several years, a lot more people have broken the sound barrier. In fact, I've observed many children's pastors and directors rivaling Yeager's speed on a daily basis. I hear them after they pass by, the only clue to their fleeting presence being a lingering sonic boom as they hurtle toward the horizon.

Let's face it: Most of us are moving too fast.

It's hard to focus on the Lord when our speed approaches Mach one! Running from program to program, Sunday to Sunday, curriculum to curriculum, conference to conference—we lose sight of *why* we do what we're doing and *whom* we're doing it for.

I'm as guilty as the next person. Maybe even *guiltier*. I rush when there's no reason. I get frustrated over the smallest things. I have a high sense of anxiety. I over-focus on my responsibilities. I develop a loss of gratitude and a sense of entitlement. And in the midst of my running and sonic booms, I lose the wonder of the Cross. And the Cross, by the way, is the primary source of our ministry and why we exist as ministers and believers.

If you find yourself thinking, "That's me, too," then welcome to the Sonic Boom Club. You have a lot of company, unfortunately.

And the first step in your healing is to say something like this: "Hi, my name is Craig, and I have a problem with sitting still."

Don't get me wrong. Staying active in ministry is a good thing for leaders. But when we zoom along at sonic speeds for too long, we're probably thinking that our source of significance flows from what we accomplish. That's why we keep our burners fired up. (But if God isn't part of our significance scenery, any hope we have of silence and solitude goes right out the picture window.)

Silence and Solitude: Do We Really Need Them?

This is one of the most difficult dilemmas for the twenty-first-century Christian: being silent and in solitude. One of my favorite verses is found in Isaiah 40:31 (GWT), which says, "The strength of those who wait with hope in the Lord will be renewed. They will soar on wings like eagles. They will run and won't become weary. They will walk and won't grow tired."

Waiting on the Lord is a key to spiritual renewal. Psalm 46:10 (NIV) reminds us to be still and focus on God: "Be still, and know that I am God; I will be exalted among the nations, I will be exalted in the earth."

I enjoy the *Message* paraphrase of this verse because I think it sums up our lives as a whole. It says, "Step out of the traffic! Take a long, loving look at me, your High God, above politics, above everything."

I like that language. "Step out of the traffic" paints a vivid picture for me. Why? Well, to explain that I have to tell you about my father-in-law...and a dog.

My father-in-law is such a dog lover that he has a reputation for picking up strays wherever he finds one. I've been riding in the car with him when he has stopped, stepped out of the car, called in a stray, and then gotten back in the car and picked up the conversation right where we'd left off. Taking care of dogs is a part of the man's nature.

I was recently driving a car behind my father-in-law when we stopped at a train crossing because a train was coming. Traffic was about twelve cars deep and four lanes wide, counting oncoming traffic. There was a street just before the train tracks, so the volume of traffic on the oncoming side was heavy. As the train was speeding by, oncoming traffic pushed forward, and people who were frustrated with the length of the train were flipping U-turns.

And there in the middle of it all sat a little dog.

Wide-eyed and frightened, the little fella was watching everything whizzing by, including the train, the U-turns, the oncoming traffic, and, moving quickly toward him, my father-in-law—who was waving a tantalizing piece of raw meat. And before you ask, I *don't* know why he had raw meat in his car.

The dog was in a panic. It appeared to me that the dog wanted to escape the onslaught of noise and hustle but was so focused on the overwhelming amount of movement around him that he was paralyzed with fear. He couldn't move.

Finally the dog, exhausted, ran to the only thing that couldn't run him over—my father-in-law. The dog found rest and safety in the man's arms, along with a nice, fresh snack.

In many ways, this is what *The Message* paraphrase is trying to communicate to us: "Step out of the traffic."

If you're anything like me, then you're also like that dog because I'm a *lot* like that dog. I get overwhelmed when there's too much swirling around in my life. I need someone to wade out into the chaos to pull me out of the traffic, out of harm's way. In a way, that person is sort of a second Holy Spirit in my life, helping me go in the right direction.

In my life that person is Mary, my wife. Who has that function in your life?

The following list is what tends to be the traffic that drives silence and solitude out of my life:

· deadlines,
· overcommitment,
· daily interruptions,
· computer failures,
· unmet expectations,
· last-minute changes, and
· general panic.

When we're stuck in traffic, we end up watching the traffic but not looking for a way out. We're like the dog, and we cower in fear. We freeze.

We need to step *out* of the traffic and take a long look at God. We need to reflect on his presence, his being, and what he does and has done for us. And the only way to achieve this is to be still and be reminded that he is, indeed, God Almighty, King of the universe, and Lover of our souls.

For most people, that sort of focused look at God happens in the context of silence and solitude. Emotional refreshment and spiritual replenishment are our reward.

Look through the New Testament, and you'll find that *Jesus never ran anywhere.* Yet there are many accounts of Jesus withdrawing from noise, withdrawing from crowds, and even separating from his friends in order to be alone.

In silence and solitude.

Silence means being quiet; *solitude* means being alone.

Some people advocate that you can have solitude even in the presence of others. I beg to differ. Being alone is simply that: *being alone.* That's why the ultimate in being alone is called "solitary confinement"—you're alone, isolated, completely away from the presence of others.

We need to practice a spiritual form of "solitary confinement" to be in the presence of our Lord. Here are some thoughts about silence and solitude.

Silence is the absence of sound. Stillness. Quietness. Jesus himself often carved out times of silent retreat because he knew the importance of taking a timeout, a pause in his ministry life. In his human nature, he, too, needed to catch his breath, recalibrate, and move on.

There is an inner silence and an outer silence. I believe you must first achieve outward silence before you can achieve inward silence. No radio, no cell phone, no interruptions, and no talking. This translates into slowing down the inner chaos that can be raging in your life. We first quiet the outside so we can quiet the inside, so God's voice can be heard above all the rest.

I've found that God does not shout; he whispers. I have a tendency to miss his voice if there is too much noise in my life.

The Bible has a lot to say about silence:

"The Lord is in his holy temple. All the earth should be silent in his presence" (Habakkuk 2:20, GWT).

"Be silent in the presence of the Almighty Lord" (Zephaniah 1:7a, GWT).

"Be silent, everyone, in the presence of the Lord, for he is coming from his holy dwelling place" (Zechariah 2:13, TEV).

"Even fools are thought to be wise when they keep silent; when they keep their mouths shut, they seem intelligent" (Proverbs 17:28, NLT).

"A time to be silent and a time to speak" (Ecclesiastes 3:7b, NIV).

The Scoop on Silence and Solitude

Solitude is temporarily choosing to be alone in order to focus on the Lord. Many people believe, wrongly, that solitude can only be achieved by conforming to monklike status and experiencing days, weeks, months, or even years of aloneness. That's simply not true. You can experience minutes or moments of solitude every day.

In our culture we have developed an aversion to solitude. We feel uneasy with being alone. In fact, we even feel uneasy if we're with a group of close friends and nobody is speaking.

Spending time in silence and solitude was likely easier for people many years ago. When there was no electricity, no phones, no classes to set up, no Game Boy, no Xbox, and no TV, they had to sit around and think up stuff to do. Today we *have* all that stuff—and much more. Now we have to find time to be silent and alone. The importance of the discipline hasn't changed, but how we accomplish it sure has.

You can have silence without solitude, but you cannot have solitude without silence. Think of it this way: Silence and solitude are complementary disciplines, and although you can accomplish solitude without silence, why would you want to? Solitude doesn't simply mean being silent, but silence is critical to the accomplishment of solitude.

For me, solitude and silence present two challenges: where and how.

Everyone asks, "Where should you go for solitude?" And everyone knows the biblical answer to this question is Carmel, California.

Carmel is the place I went to visit my grandparents every summer when I was growing up. It's the place my family enjoys spending vacations. It's one of the rare places where, when I step into the city, I physically feel fatigue melting from my body. I feel my schedule fading into the background, and I feel guilt-free.

Walking along the beach at the end of Ocean Avenue puts my whole life in perspective. We have a similar beach about thirty minutes from my house, but I don't get the same feeling of pause when I visit that stretch of sand. Why? I don't know. I don't over-analyze it; I just go to Carmel, twice a year.

What works for you? What have you tried? What will you try again?

Then there's the question of *how* you have solitude. What do you do during these moments of solitude? Great question. Since solitude is a discipline from which all others can flow, try practicing one or more of the following during your time of aloneness:

· Meditation
· Focused thinking on God
· Prayer
· Bible memory
· Bible reading
· Bible study
· Journaling
· Clearing your mind
· Being silent in God's presence

Verses about solitude:

"This is what the Lord God, the Holy One of Israel, says: 'If you come back to me and trust me, you will be saved. If you will be calm and trust me, you will be strong.' But you don't want to do that" (Isaiah 30:15).

"The Lord is kind to everyone who trusts and obeys him. It is good to wait patiently for the Lord to save us. When we are young, it is good to struggle hard and to sit silently alone, if this is what the Lord intends" (Lamentations 3:25-28, CEV).

"When you pray, go to your room and close the door. Pray privately to your Father who is with you. Your Father sees what you do in private. He will reward you" (Matthew 6:6, GWT).

Silence and solitude are both needed to revive our spirits and renew, refresh, and rejuvenate our souls. We need sleep for the body and solitude for the soul.

Recuperation Retreats:
A great way to have silence and solitude.

Sometimes you have to step outside your daily routine to find solitude. Do that and you'll be in good company. Elijah, for example, went to Mount Horeb for a silent whisper. He heard God's voice saying,

" 'Go out and stand in front of the Lord on the mountain.'

"As the Lord was passing by, a fierce wind tore mountains and shattered rocks ahead of the Lord. But the Lord was not in the wind. After the wind came an earthquake. But the Lord wasn't in the earthquake. After the earthquake there was a fire. But the Lord wasn't in the fire. And after the fire there was a quiet, whispering voice. When Elijah heard it, he wrapped his face in his coat, went out, and stood at the entrance of the cave.

"Then the voice said to him, 'What are you doing here, Elijah?' " (I Kings 19:11-13, GWT).

Habakkuk sat silently and waited for an answer from God:

"I will climb up into my watchtower now and wait to see what the Lord will say to me and how he will answer my complaint" (Habakkuk 2:1, NLT).

Paul went to the desert to be alone with God:

"I didn't go up to Jerusalem to consult with those who were apostles before I was. No, I went away into the deserts of Arabia, and then came back to the city of Damascus" (Galatians 1:17, *TLB*).

That's all well and good for Bible personalities. They apparently didn't have bosses who expected them to show up at 8 a.m. each weekday morning. But what about us today? How will we find silence and solitude?

At times I've withdrawn for periods of rest. And when I'm focusing on the Lord, I have time to slow down my heart, slow down my mind, and think about the important things—not just the urgent things. What's left when we don't have our busyness? If we're honest we may answer, "I feel empty, less fulfilled, less significant." Or if you are a real work-freak like me, you may say, "I'm wasting time."

We feel guilty when we slow down. Questions bubble up into our consciousness. *What will my staff think?* "Slacker, sloth, wimp, whiner?"

What will my boss think? "Why did I hire this guy? He's not a producer; he's not making it happen."

What will my friends think? "He doesn't really measure up; let's pray for him."

What causes you to pick up speed and refuse to pause and be still? Often it's the fear of what other people will think about your performance, right?

We need a routine practice of establishing a time and a place to give God our undivided attention—or to simply acknowledge his constant, undivided attention given to us.

As Christians, we've developed a condition known as spiritual ADD or Aloneness Deficit Disorder—our inability to be alone.

The prescription for this disorder is a strong dose of recuperation retreat. A recuperation retreat is exactly that—a time to recapture lost energy and lost values so we can focus on God. I practice three different types of retreats. Which will you plan in the weeks ahead?

· *The thirty-minute retreat.*

Here's when I take a drive. There's a great Mexican restaurant exactly thirty minutes from my office door. I occasionally get in my car, head out on the toll road by our church, and drive to the next city for a burrito at Miguel's.

I go because the burritos there are stellar, but I also go to be alone.

No radio, no phone (even if I wanted it, there's no cell coverage in the canyon)—it's like driving in a thirty-minute tunnel. During this time I memorize a verse, thank God for what he's doing and has done in my life, and...simply be still. This half-hour recalibrates my hectic day and provides a quietness for hearing God.

One of my ministry professors many years ago said something I wholeheartedly agreed with up until a few years ago: "Never do ministry alone."

The idea is to build into other people, model for them, and mentor them. I agree with all of those things. I have, however, come to realize the importance of being alone and doing stints of ministry in solitude, quietness, and aloneness. I can only lead others as far as I have gone myself. And in today's fast-paced life, a frequent retreat with my Savior makes me a better leader.

Since recuperation is really a mind-set, try the following things when you are in the middle of your hurried day.

· Find a slow driver, and pull in behind him.
· At the grocery store, locate the longest line and get in it.
· Turn off the TV at meal times.
· Seek out people who tend to move a bit slower; have lunch with them.
· Go to the DMV, just for fun!

Once you've survived one or all of those, try this next retreat.
· *The half-day retreat.*
You can do these retreats anywhere—at the beach, in the mountains, on a train, or in your home. For me, these retreats are best experienced on a plane. That's when I feel as if I'm in a bubble, a cocoon.

On the plane, I'm above the clouds, looking down on creation, seeing what God has made, and I am in *awe*. A plane ride is a great place to start a retreat. I know you're supposed to do evangelism on a plane, striking up a conversation with the person next to you no matter what.

I must be honest and tell you that I earnestly pray that *no one sits next to me on plane flights.* I reserve flight times for silence.

You see, when I'm on the ground, my life is a hurried mess. But when I'm in the air, I put on my headphones (with no music playing) and tune out the world. I focus on slowing down, pausing. I like to read from *The Message* paraphrase, maybe a verse or two, maybe an entire chapter. After digesting a few words, I sit back, close my eyes, and dwell on what I've read. I have a dialogue with my Maker. I do lots of listening, waiting in God's presence. It's a time of pause, a time of reflection, a time of renewal. Just quiet and calm before the One who loves me unconditionally.

I would encourage you to find that place, if only for two or three hours, to celebrate and reflect with the Lord. It will refresh your spirit beyond words.

· *The all-day retreat.*
Many years ago we had to plan for activity. Today we have to plan for silence. And we don't *get* silence unless we make a point of carving out a place for it.

It's likely it will take you several hours to ratchet down the pressure and to be in a spiritual place where you're ready to hear God. If you only set aside an hour for your retreat, you won't have accomplished much.

Why not take a day? An all-day retreat where you're alone before God with your Bible, a journal, and some music. A day without your cell phone, company, or responsibility. I've traditionally enhanced these retreats by fasting (as we will discuss in the next chapter).

If you experience an all-day retreat several times a year, you'll feel the difference. You'll enjoy a refreshment that's one of the best possible remedies for our Aloneness Deficit Disorder.

Just Say "No!"

Sometimes we have to say no, even to the good things. This past season, I had to write a resignation letter.

I could no longer be my twins' T-ball manager.

You see, I wanted to manage the team so I could spend time with my sons in a sport they wanted to play. One night while I was prepping all of the behind-the-scenes "stuff" a manager does, I told my kids, as they were bounding around the room, to "please leave because Daddy is trying to get this T-ball stuff together."

Huh? I paused. I'm a T-ball manager because I want to spend time with my kids. And I just kicked them out of my office so I could be a T-ball manager.

Something was wrong.

Dear Mr. Jackson,

After careful consideration and talking with my family, I realize that I won't be able to manage this year's T-ball team and will only be available as a coach.

I originally wanted to manage so I could be involved with my kids in sports. After reviewing the time requirements, I feel I'd be spending more time away from my kids organizing, planning, and leading than actually being with my kids. I experience this already with my responsibilities at Saddleback Church.

Perhaps in the future I can be a part of the leadership of the Little League. You have a great program! With my missing the first three meetings, I feel I've already failed to live up to my responsibility. After looking at the remaining dates I'm expected to be available, and matching them with my family and work calendars, I see I'll end up missing more meetings and special days.

I apologize for the late notice, but after much prayer and conversation with those most important in my life, I believe I need to be Dad instead of Manager.

God Bless,
Craig Jutila

Actually, I asked my kids whether or not they wanted me to manage their T-ball team, and they said "yes." When I told them I wouldn't be managing their T-ball team but could coach golf instead, they both said, in unison, "I want to play golf!"

Following a moment of silence, my son Alec said to me, "We want to do whatever you're doing, Dad." Translation: *We just want to spend time with you.*

Isn't that the essence of our relationship with God? Who cares what's going on, Father—we just want to spend time with you.

Dive In! (Questions for Reflection and Discussion)

1. What speeds have you reached in your "ministry flights" during the past week? Would you like to slow down—or not?

2. Why are silence and solitude difficult for so many of us? Tell about your own experience with these.

3. What kinds of retreats would work best for you? What plans could you begin making right now?

4. Make a list of some of the *good* things you may need to say "no" to in the month ahead.

5. If you are in a group, spend some time sharing about which Bible verses in this chapter spoke most powerfully to your heart. Talk about how you could apply their principles in practical ministry.

DIVING RULES AND TOOLS

Tool: *Dive log*

Spiritual Application:

A diver's log is a record of your past dives at various depths, locations, and environments. There is a place to record your activity, diving conditions, your equipment, what you saw, the temperature during the dive, the amount of weight used, and even your cumulative time underwater.

You can see the wonderful spiritual application to journaling here.

Journaling is a great way to write down how spiritually deep you feel you are now, the location of where you are spiritually, and your current environment. In the same way a diver uses a log to keep track of current and past depths achieved, record your current activity with your heavenly Father. How much weight are you using on your current dive? Has there been pain and difficulty in your life recently?

It's great to record how much weight it took to keep us buoyant in life. God offsets every hurt or pain with his loving care and grace. It's great to look back on your spiritual dive log to simply recall where you've been and what God has done and is doing in your life. When you set aside some time this week for silence and solitude, remember to record your dive.

Here is an outline of a journal page from my spiritual dive log.

Read
Chapter read today.

Reflect
Verse from chapter read today and verse to be memorized.

Respond
Journal and reflection on the passages read today. Interweaving life experience and the text.

Request
Prayers of thanks and request.

Remember
In a word or phrase, sum up your "take-away" for today. (Example: Seek the counsel of the wise for a positive surprise.)

Notes

I. Facts about sound come from Daniel A. Russell at Kettering University, at this Web site: http://www.gmi.edu/~drussell/Demos/doppler/doppler.html.

Chapter 11

Slowing and Fasting at the Same Time

Spiritual health and growth in leaders requires more than just desire. It also requires disciplines such as prayer and fasting.

Dive Tool: *Air tank*

The air tank holds high-pressure oxygen so you can breathe underwater. And without air...you guessed it...you die.

As we dive throughout our day, we occasionally run out of the heavenly air that sustains our spiritual life. We may have forgotten to check our tanks—to see that they're filled with quiet time, prayer, Scripture memory, and fasting.

I hungered for teenage revenge. Some people had double-crossed me in a house toilet-papering incident.

Now it was time for them to suffer...

You see, there was a time several years ago when toilet-papering houses was a fairly large part of my existence. A friend of mine and I were toilet-papering a girl's house (I later married the girl, by the way), and we were doing a stellar job, if I say so myself.

A few other friends showed up that night to help, and when we had finished our "Picasso," we drove to the end of the block. That's when I discovered my letterman's jacket was missing. My friends told me they'd locked it in a car sitting in the driveway of the Picasso house we'd just left.

It's an understatement to say that I was upset.

I raced back and tried to get into the car to retrieve the evidence, but to no avail. Down the street, all of my friends were laughing, and when I looked, I noticed they were also *leaving*. I jumped into my 1966 robin's-egg blue Volkswagen (hey, that color was *in* a few years ago—well, a *lot* of years ago), and I set out in hot pursuit. They escaped with ease.

So I took a gamble. There were five people in that van, so apparently they'd all met at one person's house and then driven over together. I drove to the house where I figured they'd met and, yep, there were four cars lined up in the driveway—one each for four of the gals who'd mocked me.

It was 1 a.m., but I knew a guy who lived on the street. I pounded on his door, woke him up, and asked to borrow a car jack and a lug-nut wrench. I also told him to not ask questions. He obliged.

It didn't take long to pull the tires off the car at the end of the drive—the one blocking in the other three cars. I lowered the car onto blocks—tireless—then deposited each tire on the front porch of a house in the neighborhood. When my friends got back, they found no tires, but there was a list of numbers. House numbers—though I didn't tell them that.

They never did find all the tires, and I wound up married to the girl whose house we decorated. So who's laughing now?

The point of my story: Without tires, that car wasn't going very far. The vehicle had a nice interior, a great stereo, leather seats, a spectacular sunroof, and a turbocharged engine—but it couldn't move. My friends could start the car, listen to the stereo, lean back in the leather seats, rev the engine, pop open the sunroof and enjoy the stars...but they couldn't move.

Four tires are critical to the movement of a car. And I'd suggest that silence, solitude, praying, and fasting are the four tires of our spiritual lives. We may have a fantastic interior, speak in stereo quality, feel as comfortable as leather seats, be turbocharged for God, and have a fantastic view out of our spiritual sunroof—and still not be able to move.

As a leader in ministry, you need to do more than sit around looking good; you need to *move*. If you aren't going anywhere, what's there to follow? Your spiritual well-being and growth is important not just to you but also to the people God has placed around you—people who look to you for direction and guidance.

We've already explored the importance of spending time in silence and solitude. They're important when it comes to moving toward Christlikeness. But I don't think they're enough. They're some of the tire rubber we need under us, but there's a need for more.

We also need to practice a routine time of praying and fasting.

Is Fasting Really for Today?

I became a Christian during my junior year of high school. After high school, I attended Biola University and Talbot Seminary. Throughout my years attending church as a teen, and later as an adult, and through all of the chapels in college and all of the Bible classes, I can't remember ever hearing a message on fasting.

Not growing up in the church, I viewed fasting as an Old Testament law that we just don't practice anymore, kind of like animal sacrifice. It seemed a bit odd. Giving up eating for some spiritual purpose didn't sound like much fun. What was the point?

It's embarrassing to say, but until a few years ago, I'd never fasted. Then a critical injury to one of my sons caused me to look into every possible way to get God's attention. Occasionally God puts us on our backs so we have to look up to him, and this was that sort of experience for me. I wanted more than to "just pray." I wanted more than one or two people praying. I wanted every available prayer resource brought to bear on my son's plight during this time of family crisis.

It's interesting to note that Jesus didn't quite take the same approach as I did to fasting. In fact, he *assumes* that we all fast and pray routinely. Take a look at what he said...

"When you fast, don't make it obvious, as the hypocrites do, who try to look pale and disheveled so people will admire them for their fasting. I assure you, that is the only reward they will ever get. But when you fast, comb your hair and wash your face. Then no one will suspect you are fasting, except your Father, who knows what you do in secret. And your Father, who knows all secrets, will reward you" (Matthew 6:16-18, NLT).

Did you notice? *When* you fast. Not if, *when*. Our Creator assumes we fast. He went so far as to address our motives and how we look during a fast. I like the *Message* paraphrase of these verses; it really makes the text come alive:

"When you practice some appetite-denying discipline to better concentrate on God, don't make a production out of it. It might turn you into a small-time celebrity but it won't make you a saint. If you 'go into training' inwardly, act normal outwardly. Shampoo and comb your hair, brush your teeth, wash your face. God doesn't require attention-getting devices. He won't overlook what you are doing; he'll reward you well" (Matthew 6:16-18, *The Message*).

Did you know that fasting is mentioned more times in the Bible than baptism? Baptism and church seem to be synonymous, yet fasting rarely appears in a sermon or seminar.

The Old Testament patriarchs talked and wrote about fasting, and the children of Israel practiced it. New Testament believers observed Jesus fasting as an example for them.

And there's no question that we believers today are to be fasting.

Why, When, and How?

Fasting, according to the Bible, means to voluntarily reduce or abstain from eating for a specific time and purpose.

For believers, fasting shouldn't be just a religious exercise. Instead, it should be a spiritual dynamic by which abstaining from food becomes a key to opening ourselves to the power of God and bringing ourselves into humble submission to him. Fasting isn't just about abstaining from food but from *anything* that hinders our communication with God. Fasting means to do without, or to practice self-denial.

Fasting isn't a "trick" to get God's attention or some superstitious behavior practiced by overly religious people. However, I do believe that fasting releases God's supernatural power. It's a tool we can use when there's opposition to God's will. Satan would like nothing better than to cause division, discouragement, defeat, depression, and doubt among us. "So we fasted and earnestly prayed that our God would take care of us, and he heard our prayer" (Ezra 8:23, NLT).

Fasting isn't a way of seeking God's blessings as much as it is a means of seeking God himself. Fasting isn't a practice for super saints, it's not a way to twist God's arm, and it's not a magical formula for getting through to God. It's a spiritual practice that should be observed by all believers as a means of staying spiritually healthy. Jesus expected his followers to fast, and he said God rewards it.

The most common occurrences of fasting in the Bible were for personal or public repentance. Israel fasted each year on the Day of Atonement. Nehemiah, David, Jesus, Anna, Paul, and Barnabas participated in normal fasts, abstaining from all food but not from water. Daniel entered into a partial fast, restricting his diet without totally abstaining from food. Queen Esther practiced an absolute fast, avoiding all food and water for three days before going to see the king.

A word about fasting: It's not easy.

When your stomach is growling and people around you are eating like there's no tomorrow, you feel powerfully tempted to "take a little bite" and indulge.

As a fast day lingers on (and I choose the word *linger* very carefully here), hunger pains increase. You spend more time thinking about those noises and pains in your stomach than what is going on around you.

For me, whenever my stomach growls, I stop and pray. Not the fall-on-your-knees-tear-your-garment-cry-out-to-God sort of prayer, but a quiet prayer. Remember, Jesus said to not let anyone know you're fasting. I just stop for a moment and pray. Hunger acts as an internal "prayer alarm clock" that God sets and rings for me. Those hunger pains remind me of God and why I'm in ministry. They remind me to focus my prayers and not rush through my day.

Biblical Types of Fasting

There are at least five types of fasts found in Scripture:

The Normal Fast

Abstaining from all food but not water. This is the fast Jesus observed in the wilderness.

"For forty wilderness days and nights he was tested by the Devil. He ate nothing during those days, and when the time was up he was hungry" (Luke 4:2, *The Message*).

The Complete Fast

Eating and drinking nothing for the entire time.

"Assemble all the Jews in Susa. Fast for me: Do not eat or drink at all for three entire days. My servants and I will also fast. After that, I will go to the king, even if it is against a royal decree. If I die, I die" (Esther 4:16, GWT).

The Partial Fast

Eliminating certain foods or specific meals, as Daniel did after he received a vision from the Lord.

"I didn't eat any good-tasting food. No meat or wine entered my mouth" (Daniel 10:3a, GWT).

The Private Fast

Keeping it secret that you are fasting.

"When you fast, don't make it obvious, as the hypocrites do, who try to look pale and disheveled so people will admire them for their fasting. I assure you, that is the only reward they will ever get. But when you fast, comb your hair and wash your face. Then no one will suspect you are fasting, except your Father, who knows what you do in secret. And your Father, who knows all secrets, will reward you" (Matthew 6:16-18, NLT).

The Public Fast

Fasting as a group.

"Schedule a time to fast! Call for an assembly! Gather the leaders and everyone who lives in the land. Bring them to the temple of the Lord your God, and cry to the Lord for help" (Joel 1:14, GWT).

Once I realized the cleansing power and focus fasting can bring to me personally, I began fasting for our children's staff here at Saddleback.

Now, once a quarter, we have a PFD (prayer fast day). Each member of our team spends the entire twenty-four hours in a normal fast. I send out a prayer and fasting focus to our team so we can be unified in our hearts and minds. Our PFDs are a time of praying for our leadership, our children, our team, and other needs as they arise. These have brought our team together spiritually and replenished our spiritual tanks. We've seen God move in ways that we never saw before.

We're healthier, happier, and have a greater faith in our God. We don't use fasting as a leverage to get God to do something that is not in accord with his will. We simply surrender our agendas to him. We're reminded in Proverbs 16:3 (GWT) to "entrust your efforts to the Lord, and your plans will succeed."

I've found that it's not so much about what we did or didn't eat, or how long we went without eating, but simply about our hearts—that's what's important. After all, "it is out of the abundance of the heart that the mouth speaks" (Luke 6:45b, New Revised Standard Version). "Above all else, guard your heart, for it affects everything you do" (Proverbs 4:23, NLT). If you want a healthy heart, you need to watch more than your cheese intake; you need to watch your spiritual intake as well.

"That is why the Lord says, 'Turn to me now, while there is time! Give me your hearts. Come with fasting, weeping, and mourning. Don't tear your clothing in your grief; instead, tear your hearts.' Return to the Lord your God, for he is gracious and merciful. He is not easily angered. He is filled with kindness and is eager not to punish you" (Joel 2:12-13, NLT).

What am I suggesting you do as a leader in ministry?

I'm suggesting that you build into your life those things that will make you healthier in your leadership, more impactful in your teaching, stronger in your skills. The church needs you hitting on all cylinders, with all four tires under you.

Fasting is one of those things that gives you health and power.

I know personally the power of a fasting. Because of the profound impact in my son's life, in my life as a ministry leader and a follower of Christ, and in my family life, I searched the Scriptures to understand this spiritual practice. The benefits I've received from focused prayer and fasting have been awesome.

If I could put a word picture to it, I'd say it's like a spiritual "spring cleaning." Our body is God's temple, and we need to maintain its condition. That's why the Apostle Paul tells us to honor God with our bodies:

"Do you not know that your body is a temple of the Holy Spirit, who is in you, whom you have received from God? You are not your own; you were bought at a price. Therefore honor God with your body" (I Corinthians 6:19-20, NIV).

After a two-day fast, my mind is more alert. Once I start eating again, my thoughts are more focused. I have more "God thoughts" than "Craig thoughts," and I have more empathy and concern for those around me.

Now, I don't want to sound like a dietician here—I'm not one. But for me, I'm physically healthier as a result of my fasting routine. For example, I used to have rigorous bouts with canker sores. I'd have up to six or seven sores in my mouth at one time.

With an exercise program and routine fasting, I've seen the canker sore problem all but disappear. I simply feel better physically since I've practiced a regular fasting schedule. Other benefits that I wrote down in my journal one day include...

Food becomes more "fresh," and I appreciate each bite.

I more fully enjoy the basic pleasures of life.

I appreciate what I have, not what I don't have.

My thinking is more focused.

I learn to live without.

My mind is constantly on target with what I'm praying about.

I develop greater discipline.

What About Related Disciplines?

Discipline is a word we don't like to use. When I see that word, I see...
work,
sacrifice,
focus,
pain, and
perseverance.

Words we tend to *like* include words like...
relax,
chill,
take a break,
quit, and
give up.

Discipline Needs a New PR Campaign

Discipline has received a bad rap over the centuries, but nothing great was ever achieved without it. Bringing your body, mind, will, and emotions under control for a focused time of "God thoughts" is *essential* to a healthy self—and a healthy ministry team.

Fasting is a piece of the answer, but only a piece. Certain other disciplines—such as prayer, Scripture memory, and meditation—must accompany fasting.

Let's focus on prayer. Most believers manage to pray sometime during the day, but when accompanied by fasting, prayer becomes a powerful, potent tool.

While my wife, Mary, was praying with our twin sons, Alec and Cameron, she stumbled across a teachable moment. Mary had prayed first. She had prayed for our kids and other family needs, and then she let Alec pray. His prayer was right on the money; thankful, heartfelt, and genuine.

At one point Alec prayed something that really hit home with Mary, and she said, "Yes, Lord!" Alec stopped and said, "Mommy, what does it mean when you say, 'Yes, Lord'?"

Up until this point, he had only heard the person praying say, "Yes, Lord." The words were out of context for him. To Alec it sounded like Mary was cutting off his prayer.

Mary explained to Alec that when she said, "Yes, Lord!" she was agreeing with his prayer. She was 100 percent behind what he prayed. She was giving him a kind of verbal high five.

Alec took in this whole conversation. Then it was Cameron's turn to pray. He got to the point where he was thanking God for his family. "Thank you for Mommy and Daddy and Alec..."

And that's when Alec interjected his own "Yes, Lord!"

Listen, if you're serious about living a life pleasing to God, then I'd offer a big "Yes, Lord!" as you add a discipline of fasting in your life, and accompany it with prayer, Scripture memory, and meditation.

When I take my kids to school in the morning, we often pop in a Jana Alayra CD and sing like there's no tomorrow. One of the songs that Ron and Jana have written is called "Down on My Knees." See if you can relate to some of the lyrics:

If I lose the wonder in my heart
Help me to remember who you are
If I forget the meaning of the cross
Help me to remember what it cost
How amazing that you died for me
So I can be set forever free
You gave your life
So I will never die
There's a place I need to be
Where the truth is plain to see
I gotta go down, gotta go down
Gotta go down on my knees

There's a place I need to go
Where mercy and forgiveness flow
I gotta go down, gotta go down
Gotta go down on my knees.[1]

Bottom line: There's a place you need to be if you want to see truth. It's on your knees before God.

When Is It Appropriate to Fast? Consider—

When waiting for guidance

"One day as they were worshiping God—they were also fasting as they waited for guidance—the Holy Spirit spoke: 'Take Barnabas and Saul and commission them for the work I have called them to do.'

"So they commissioned them. In that circle of intensity and obedience, of fasting and praying, they laid hands on their heads and sent them off" (Acts 13:2-3, *The Message*).

When selecting leadership

"Paul and Barnabas handpicked leaders in each church. After praying—their prayers intensified by fasting—they presented these new leaders to the Master to whom they had entrusted their lives" (Acts 14:23, *The Message*).

When in distress

"One of my brothers, Hanani, came with certain men from Judah; and I asked them about the Jews that survived, those who had escaped the captivity, and about Jerusalem. They replied, 'The survivors there in the province who escaped captivity are in great trouble and shame; the wall of Jerusalem is broken down, and its gates have been destroyed by fire.'

"When I heard these words I sat down and wept, and mourned for days, fasting and praying before the God of heaven" (Nehemiah 1:2-5, NRSV).

When asking for a "miracle answer"

"Saul got up from the ground and opened his eyes, but he could not see. So those with Saul took his hand and led him into Damascus. For three days Saul could not see and did not eat or drink" (Acts 9:8-9).

"In a vision he has seen a man named Ananias place his hands on him to restore his sight" (Acts 9:12, GWT).

When in a crisis

"They mourned, cried, and fasted until evening because Saul, his son Jonathan, the Lord's army, and the nation of Israel had been defeated in battle" (2 Samuel 1:12, GWT).

When needing a safe journey

"Then I announced a fast there at the Ahava River so that we might humble ourselves in the presence of our God to ask him for a safe journey for ourselves, for our little ones, and for all our goods" (Ezra 8:21, GWT).

When faced with an attack

The Moabites, Ammonites, and some of the Meunites were planning an attack against Jehoshaphat. Jehoshaphat's first response was to gather the people of Judah to pray for a fast. "Frightened, Jehoshaphat decided to ask for the Lord's help. He announced a fast throughout Judah" (2 Chronicles 20:3, GWT).

Fasting Precautions

In the same way I'm not a dietician, I'm also not a medical doctor. If you're going to add a routine of fasting for your spiritual health, it's smart to ask what it will do to your physical health. There are some medical conditions that would indicate that fasting should be undertaken very gradually, if at all.

There are spiritual cautions for fasting too.

For example, there's a danger that we may turn fasting into an end in itself. Just like any spiritual discipline, we may perceive what we're doing as the end-all result. Fasting can become an icon of external practice rather than internal passion, and we can end up favoring a habit without involving the heart.

The Pharisee in Luke 18:11-14 bragged to God that he fasted twice a week. Actually, *most* Pharisees fasted twice a week, usually on the second and fifth days of the week. Those two days happened to be the major days for the Jewish market. That meant the city was packed with people. This account tells us that the Pharisee was praying loudly so that a nearby tax collector could hear him, no doubt on one of the days set aside in the Law to fast.

And why not? The religious leaders would have the largest audiences on these days. This is a great example of habit without heart.

Fasting is meant for focusing on God, drawing closer to him. Fasting is not as much about food as about focus. It's not so much about saying "no" to the body as saying "yes" to the Spirit. It's not so much about doing without as looking within.

Fasting is an outward response to an inward attitude and heart for God. God asked for the heartfelt love of his people:

"Say to all your people and your priests, 'During those seventy years of exile, when you fasted and mourned in the summer and at the festival in early autumn, was it really for me that you were fasting?' " (Zechariah 7:5, NLT).

As you can tell, I'm all for fasting. And I invite you to approach the Lord this way, too, whenever it would seem appropriate in your life.

As for me, I don't see how I could cope without this spiritual discipline. My son has had over fourteen eye surgeries to date, due to an injury he sustained over two years ago. I've fasted each time he's had a surgery or procedure.

To this date, and through God's power, my son's recovery has been literally miraculous—and all surgeries have gone better than expected.

I believe God's power is at work. I believe the effective prayer of a righteous person accomplishes much, and I believe in the power of fasting. The doctors can't explain it, but I can.

I've lived the effects of fasting and have seen the effects of fasting and prayer. A child's eye healed. A husband returning to his wife. A children's ministry crashing through quitting points because of quarterly prayer-fast days.

I've seen our children's attendance grow by 19 percent because of praying and fasting. I've seen a growing heart for kids in our entire volunteer leadership team because of focused fasting. I've seen my team pursue ministry not as a job but as a calling, and I've seen miracles, growth, health, faith, wonder, power, and purpose because of fasting.

For me, seeing is believing.

What do you see?

Dive In! (Questions for Reflection and Discussion)

1. What is the longest period of time you've gone without food, but not by choice? How did you feel?

2. What is your *experience* with fasting? What are your *beliefs* about fasting?

3. What is the most important or inspiring thing you've learned about fasting in this chapter?

4. Have you ever felt that fasting was just an outdated "Old Testament thing"? What would be your own argument for New Testament believers to fast today?

5. In your group, share your prayer concerns. Do any of these seem to call for a period of fasting among you?

DIVING RULES AND TOOLS

Tool: *Air tank*

Spiritual Application:
The air tank holds high-pressure oxygen so you can breathe underwater for extended periods of time. Without air, there's not only no diving but there's also no life.

Some people run out of air during their dive, and that's a disaster unless someone comes alongside them and gives them the needed oxygen.

As we dive throughout our day, we occasionally run out of the "spiritual air" that sustains us. We may have forgotten to check our tanks, which need to be filled with regular, disciplined quiet time; prayer; Scripture memory; and fasting. These disciplines are our air for diving into life and ministry, day after day.

Notes

1. "Down on My Knees," words and music by Ron and Jana Alayra, from the *Believin' On* CD. Used by permission of the authors.

Chapter 12

More Caught Than Taught

Dive Rule: *Learn from a master diver.*

No matter how long you've been diving, there's always someone who's better than you—and you can learn a lot by watching that diver. How the diver prepares. How the diver moves. How the diver makes decisions. If you want to become an excellent diver, you need an excellent teacher who'll model excellence.

The late comedienne Gilda Radner told a story about her cousin's dog...

It wasn't an expensive dog, and it was pregnant. It apparently wasn't a very fast dog, either, because it ended up getting in the way of a lawn mower.

The dog lost its two hind legs but was saved when the owners rushed her to a veterinarian who gave the owners two choices: He could stitch up the dog and let it live with only two legs, or he could put the dog down. If the dog was stitched up, the puppies she carried would be born, no problem. If the dog died, then, obviously, the puppies would die too.

Radner's cousin told the vet to stitch up the dog, and here's what happened...

"So the vet sewed up her backside," writes Radner, "and over the next week the dog learned to walk. She didn't spend any time worrying, she just learned to walk by taking two steps in the front and flipping up her backside, and then taking two steps and flipping up her backside again."[1]

The surgically transformed dog gave birth to six perfectly healthy puppies. But here's the amazing thing: After she nursed and weaned the puppies, they learned to walk—and they all walked exactly like their mother! They each took two steps with their front paws and then flipped their backsides forward.

Why did these healthy puppies walk like their mother? Because she was their model for "how to walk." You see, *modeling* right behavior has more impact than *talking* about it.

Here's the reality of your life: You're a leader. And though many people aren't listening to you, everyone is watching you.

Everything we've addressed in this book culminates here. Few people remember what we say, but they all seem to remember what we do. They take in our behavior; they become reflections of who we are, how we do ministry, how we balance our lives, and how we submit to the leading of Christ.

Knowing this to be true, we need to surrender our lives daily to allow the power of Christ to consume us. The Apostle Paul reminds us...

"Therefore I urge you, brethren, by the mercies of God, to present your bodies a living and holy sacrifice, acceptable to God, which is your spiritual service of worship" (Romans 12:1, NASB).

It has been said that children aren't all that good when it comes to listening to their parents, but children never fail to watch and imitate parents. And since most things are caught rather than taught, it's important for all leaders to model right behavior.

That's the challenge we face. Let's look at five key areas in which we can help those we lead to "learn to walk like us" (remember those puppies!) through intentional modeling.

Always Be Modeling

The master salesman's mantra is "Always be closing." Similarly, those of us who lead teams and work with children can have a watchword phrase: "Always be modeling."

The truth is that we *are* always modeling, whether we know it or not. What we *are* is being conveyed to *whomever we are with*. The key is to make sure we are conveying the best of us—conveying to others what the Spirit is growing in us: the likeness of our Lord Jesus.

So we ask ourselves daily, "What one thing do I want my staff to catch from me today?"

Maybe it's managing time in a more strategic way. Maybe it's reflecting a positive emotional intelligence. Maybe it's making wise choices or controlling the flow. Whatever it is, make sure that today you model it wisely. Such things are more caught than taught.

And the deep learning that comes from modeling happens best in an atmosphere that's fragrant with patience.

People who plant Moso bamboo know all about patience. After a plant is placed in the ground, it can be two or three years before any visible growth occurs. The plant doesn't get taller. It doesn't flower. It doesn't send up new sprouts.

But you still have to care for it. You have to water and fertilize it regularly, tend the soil, protect it from pests and predators—and for what? You're still looking at the same little plant you put in the ground years before.

But then, as if by magic, the bamboo plant suddenly begins to grow—and grow rapidly. Some plants have been clocked at a growth rate of nearly two and a half feet per day, reaching a full height of up to ninety feet within six weeks!

But there's no magic involved. The secret of the Moso's rapid and sturdy growth is what has happened during the years when its caretaker saw no results at all. During that time the plant was establishing deep, solid roots, creating a firm foundation for growth.

The truth is that the Moso plant can't grow tall without deep, solid, strong roots. If we "caretakers" of God's people don't invest our best time carefully tending

Manage Your Time

Your Priorities

I recently came across an article that explored how children lose out on their parents' time due to the demands of the American workplace.

The article claimed that kids are paying a high price.

Experts from a range of fields confirmed what you and I already know: The time children spend with their parents is vital to every aspect of children's healthy development. If kids don't get enough time with parents, children suffer when it comes to thinking and coping skills, school performance, and even physical health.

But even as new evidence mounts that parents should be home more, focusing on children, Americans are working longer and longer hours. And workplaces often don't recognize parents' need for flexibility to care for their children.

So does working get in the way of being a good parent? Does being a good parent mean you're bound to run into trouble at work? Obviously, it's a balancing act that many parents have to manage daily.

How the balancing act is handled depends on parents' priorities.

What are your priorities as a person and as a leader? Whether or not you're a parent, it's a question you have to answer—and your actions *are* your answer. What comes first in your life? What comes last?

Something I've been learning lately about ministry is that none of us really *goes* to work; we're *surrounded* by it. Isn't it true? For example, I came home the other day with my briefcase. I sat down at the counter, and, without saying a word, I pulled out my laptop, turned it on, and started typing.

My kids came over and asked me what I was doing. I told them, "Daddy had so much to do today that he couldn't get it all done, so he had to bring the work home."

My kids thought about that for a moment and then said, "Well, Daddy, maybe they could move you to a slower group at work."

If we're honest, how many of us would admit to wanting to be in a "slower group" at church or at home?

Clearly, whatever we value, that's where our time will go. With this in mind, let's take a moment to focus on our children. Dr. James Dobson, in his book *Bringing Up Boys*, says, "This disengagement of parents in our fast-paced and dizzying world will show up repeatedly in our discussion of boys. It is *the* underlying problem plaguing children today."[2]

Closely observe Dobson's language here: "fast-paced and dizzying." When we're moving at such a fast pace, we tend to dishonor those closest to us, namely our children. Life—excuse me—*church* gets so out of balance that we lose sight of what is dearest to us. We are modeling not only wrong priorities for those we lead but also poor parenting.

This past week I was moving so fast with work-related issues that I offended both of my children. My wife picked up the kids after school and met me at Sportmart to buy some cleats and other things needed for T-ball. I was in a hurry to get to a meeting, and I "rushed" the experience. (Have you been there?) I chose the wrong words and the wrong tone. Later, I had to apologize to all of them. My meeting at church was more "important" than the experience with my children. How tragic.

We can rightfully discipline our children, or we can make them frustrated and angry. As the Scripture says, "Fathers, don't exasperate your children by coming down hard on them. Take them by the hand and lead them in the way of the Master" (Ephesians 6:4, *The Message*).

Here's a little experiment you can try at home. Several times this week, ask your kids, "Can I play with you?" See how many times they say, "In just a minute."

Managing our time would be a great model for our children.

And if you don't have children, you still need to manage your priorities in such a way that you have close, loving relationships with people who know they can trust you to do what you say you'll do, when you say you'll do it. Who in your life knows that you love them more than work?

Observe Teachable Moments

Your Plan

Do you look for "teachable moments" throughout your day?

Depending on your observation skills, they are probably all around you. You could be leading an elementary art class, mentoring and encouraging a new staff member who feels overwhelmed, or just chatting with a fellow teacher who congratulated you on a sticky situation you handled with tact. Take advantage of each of these moments—just as Jesus took advantage of the teachable moments around him.

When an opportunity arose, Jesus taught, and people learned. The greatest teacher demonstrated how to teach and lead as he intended—by engaging people where they are, in the moment.

Jesus never seemed rushed when he paused to teach people during teachable moments. He asked a question or offered a few words that zinged to the heart of the matter. He connected with people and modeled what they needed to learn.

How does your team learn to forgive?

They watch you forgive.

How does your team learn how to give?

They watch you give.

How does your team learn how to serve?

They watch you serve.

We have a friend whose son was pretty strong-willed when the boy was younger. He would hold his breath if he didn't get his way. In fact, he would hold his breath until he *passed out* if he didn't get his way.

Imagine! You're at Target, the kid doesn't get his way, so he holds his breath. Now you have a "clean up on aisle 5" situation that's going to get everyone's attention.

Initially, this behavior thoroughly alarmed the boy's mother. I remember asking her, "So what do you do when he does his breath thing?" She told me that she had started carrying a squirt bottle around with her. When he would hold his breath, she would just squirt him in the face, and he would come around.

Now *that's* a teachable moment. Those moments are literally all around us and often arise when somebody is pushing the limits.

We all push the boundaries occasionally, though we all need boundaries. As a younger children's pastor several years ago, I thought empowerment meant getting leaders in place and then letting them go. On the contrary, that's not empowerment; it's just dumb.

Empowerment isn't chaos. It consists of delineating well-defined boundaries and offering proper training with lots of encouragement. And when people push those boundaries—as they often will—a leader uses these teachable moments.

Let me "kidicize" this for you a bit. Children have a great need to know where behavioral boundaries are and to be sure about who has the courage to enforce them. Years ago, during the early days of the progressive-education movement, an enthusiastic theorist decided to take down the chain-link fence that surrounded the nursery school yard. He thought the children would feel more freedom of movement without that visible barrier surrounding them.

When the fence was removed, however, the boys and girls huddled near the center of the play yard. Not only did they not wander away, but they didn't even venture to the edge of the grounds.

There's security for us in defined boundaries. That's why a child will push a parent to the point of exasperation at times. Children are testing the resolve of the mother or father and exploring the limits of their world.

Bottom line: We all push the limits a bit. And when we do, teachable moments arise. The wise leader is ready, at just that moment, to engage and teach.

Decide to Play

Your Participation

Make a decision to have fun and play with your team. Your whimsical spirit and ability to play is more than important; it's critical to the health of your team.

Our children's ministry staff retreats have usually been dedicated to planning, strategizing, and vision casting. This past year, however, I reorganized the entire three-day retreat. The agenda, with the exception of one meeting, was "play." It was one of the best retreats we ever had and cemented us as a team.

The Bible not only condones this type of behavior but it mandates it. Take a look at Ecclesiastes 8:15 (NLT): "So I recommend having fun, because there is nothing better for people to do in this world than to eat, drink, and enjoy life. That way they will experience some happiness along with all the hard work God gives them."

The staff that plays together stays together. So have fun—as you lead the team.

Encourage Your Team

Your Praise

My favorite definition of *encouragement* is "to give courage or confidence to other people, and to raise their hopes." The Bible says,

"Think of ways to encourage one another to outbursts of love and good deeds" (Hebrews 10:24, NLT).

How can we encourage our team? How about a hug, a high five, or a handshake? We need to cheer others on!

Some environments don't ever promote encouragement. You're just sort of expected to show up and do the work, and when you do it, well, that's expected too. The most encouraging thing that happens is not hearing from your boss. You get introduced to "upper management" only when you've blown it somehow.

That's not encouragement, of course; it's fear.

As leaders we need to model encouragement on a consistent, daily basis. An encouraging word, an encouraging e-mail, an encouraging note—these little things make a huge difference. The Bible says to encourage one another as long as it is called today. Well...*it's today!*

For those occasional times you're upset at poor performance, here are a couple of reminders:

· *When you're angry, remember:*

"A gentle answer will calm a person's anger, but an unkind answer will cause more anger" (Proverbs 15:1).

· *When you're frustrated , remember:*

"Losing your temper causes a lot of trouble, but staying calm settles arguments" (Proverbs 15:18, CEV).

· *When someone on your team fails, remember:*

"Careless words stab like a sword, but the words of wise people bring healing" (Proverbs 12:18, GWT).

· *When somebody on the team is discouraged, remember:*

"Kind words are good medicine, but deceitful words can really hurt" (Proverbs 15:4, CEV).

Don't know exactly how to encourage others? Hey, that may be the case if you've never received much encouragement yourself. Here are a few verbal starters that can help prime your encouragement pump:

Great job!
I'm glad you're on the team.
I'm glad I get to serve with you.
Thank you for keeping your workplace neat.
That's a great plan!
I like your smile.
You are God's gift to this team.
I trust you.

You are a great leader.
That was an awesome performance.
I am proud of you.
I am happy for you.

Learn From Difficulty

Your Perspective

We've spent time on this subject in a previous chapter, so I'll only make one point about difficulty here. When trouble hits us as leaders, we are transformed. To the very bone, we are transformed by the hurt and pain of the circumstances that surround us.

As leaders we come through difficulties in our lives with a new perspective, a new heart, and new eyes. Our perspective changes, and our lives are altered. With these changes, hopefully for the better, we begin to model our leadership differently. We model a "post-crisis character" that others can learn from as well.

I've learned many things by going through difficulties and crises in my life...

I've learned that, regardless of what I think, God is in control.

I've learned that God can perform miracles in lives and families because he is just that big.

I've learned that hope is all I need.

I've learned to focus on the big stuff and forget the small stuff.

I've learned that most stuff is small stuff.

I've learned the value of perspective.

I've learned that my family has grown closer together in the midst of pain and tragedy.

I've learned that I am not the best parent in the world.

I've learned to ask five-year-olds for forgiveness when I was wrong.

I've learned from difficulty, and so have my family, friends, and co-workers.

to, protecting, watering, and fertilizing our relationship with God and our team members, we may never see visible growth to maturity.

Yet the most encouraging thing of all is to know that it is not ultimately our work. It is God's work. And he promises to complete it. All praise to him!

"Being confident of this, that he who began a good work in you will carry it on to completion until the day of Christ Jesus" (Philippians 1:6, NIV).

Dive In! (Questions for Reflection and Discussion)

1. Recall the puppy story at the beginning of this chapter. What is your own most memorable modeling experience?

2. How well are you doing at managing work and family time? What adjustments would you like to make in the coming weeks?

3. What teachable moment has been a powerful learning experience in your own spiritual growth? Think about *why*.

4. Do you agree that "play" is as important as I suggest it is? Why or why not? What are your thoughts about "playing together as a team"?

5. Think back through the times of serious difficulty in your life. What key things have you learned? How have you grown through these trying times?

6. How do you answer the question "What one thing do I want my staff to catch from me today?"

DIVING RULES AND TOOLS

Rule: *Learn from a master diver.*

Spiritual Application:
No leader is perfect. Every leader needs to grow. But growth doesn't happen by accident—it requires our active participation. We need mentors in our lives as leaders, people who'll encourage us, challenge us, and model the skills and attitudes we need to learn. And at all times, we need to be alert to our ultimate mentor and Lord—Jesus.

Notes
1. Gilda Radner, *It's Always Something* (New York: Simon & Schuster, 1989), 268-269.

2. Dr. James Dobson, *Bringing Up Boys* (Wheaton, IL: Tyndale House, 2001), 36.